The Effects of a Choice Automobile Insurance Plan on Insurance Costs and Compensation

An Updated Analysis

Stephen J. Carroll

Allan F. Abrahamse

T0306664

RAND

The Institute for Civil Justice

THE INSTITUTE FOR CIVIL JUSTICE

The mission of the Institute for Civil Justice is to improve private and public decisionmaking on civil legal issues by supplying policymakers and the public with the results of objective, empirically based, analytic research. The ICJ facilitates change in the civil justice system by analyzing trends and outcomes, identifying and evaluating policy options, and bringing together representatives of different interests to debate alternative solutions to policy problems. The Institute builds on a long tradition of RAND research characterized by an interdisciplinary, empirical approach to public policy issues and rigorous standards of quality, objectivity, and independence.

ICJ research is supported by pooled grants from corporations, trade and professional associations, and individuals; by government grants and contracts; and by private foundations. The Institute disseminates its work widely to the legal, business, and research communities, and to the general public. In accordance with RAND policy, all Institute research products are subject to peer review before publication. ICJ publications do not necessarily reflect the opinions or policies of the research sponsors or of the ICJ Board of Overseers.

BOARD OF OVERSEERS

Bill Wagner, Wagner, Vaughan & McLaughlin

Paul C. Weiler, Henry J. Friendly Professor of Law, Harvard University Law School

PREFACE

Escalating auto insurance premiums have been a major public policy issue at the state level for the last three decades. *No-fault* auto insurance, born in the 1960s, was one response. It offered cost savings and speedier, more certain compensation to auto accident victims. But because it required that some claimants give up rights to seek compensation through the courts, many states found it an unappealing alternative. *Choice* auto insurance addresses this concern by giving drivers the option of selecting a somewhat modified version of their state's current auto insurance plan or a no-fault plan. In prior work, the Institute for Civil Justice used data on auto insurance claims closed in 1987 to estimate how a choice plan would affect auto insurance costs in each state. At the request of the Joint Economic Committee of the United States Congress, we extended the analysis to estimate the effects of a variant of that plan. This report uses more recent data for claims closed in 1992 to update those estimates .

The Institute for Civil Justice has been conducting research on auto insurance issues since its inception in 1979. This study will be of interest to policymakers in each state concerned with insurance matters, to insurers, and to consumers.

For information about the Institute for Civil Justice, contact

Dr. Deborah Hensler, Director
Institute for Civil Justice
RAND
1700 Main Street, P.O. Box 2138
Santa Monica, CA 90407-2138
TEL: (310) 393-0411 x7803
Internet: Deborah_Hensler@rand.org

A profile of the ICJ, abstracts of its publications, and ordering information can also be found on RAND's home page on the World Wide Web at http://www.rand.org/ and on RAND's gopher server at info.rand.org.

CONTENTS

Preface . . . v

Figures . . . ix

Tables . . . xi

Summary . . . xiii

Acknowledgments . . . xvii

Acronyms . . . xix

1. INTRODUCTION . . . 1
   - Purposes and Scope of This Study . . . 1
   - The Choice Plan . . . 1
   - Key Findings . . . 4
   - Scope and Limitations . . . 5
   - Organization of the Discussion . . . 7

2. RESEARCH APPROACH . . . 9
   - Data . . . 9
   - Estimating Compensation Costs Under the Current System . . . 10
   - Uninsured Accident Victims . . . 11
   - Insured Accident Victims . . . 12
   - Estimating the Distribution of Accident Victims . . . 13
   - Estimating Compensation Costs Under the Choice System . . . 14
   - Accidents Not Involving an ANF Insured . . . 15
   - Uninsured Victims of Accidents Caused by an ANF Insured . . . 15
   - Accident Victims Covered by ANF . . . 15
   - Victims Covered by the Modified Current System Injured in Accidents Caused by an ANF Insured . . . 15
   - Break-Even Personal Injury Premiums . . . 17
   - Relative Savings on Compensation Costs . . . 17
   - Relative Savings on Total Premiums . . . 18

3. RESULTS AND SENSITIVITY ANALYSIS . . . 19
   - Overview . . . 19
   - The Effects of the Choice Plan on Costs . . . 20
   - The Effects of the Choice Plan on Compensation . . . 23
   - Sensitivity Analyses . . . 25
     - Sensitivity to Assumed Parameters . . . 25
     - Sensitivity to Data Outliers . . . 26
     - Sensitivity to Other Assumptions . . . 28

4. CONCLUSIONS . . . 35

Appendix
- A. TECHNICAL DETAILS . . . 37
- B. WHY THE 1992 RESULTS DIFFER FROM THE 1987 RESULTS . . . 41

Bibliography . . . 45

ICJ Publications . . . 47

FIGURES

3.1. Effects of Choice Plan on Compensation Outcomes in California 24
3.2. Relative Savings for Drivers Who Switch If Half of Insured Drivers Switch to ANF: Smallest, Nominal, and Largest Percent Savings 29
3.3. Relative Savings for Drivers If All Insured Drivers Switch to ANF: Smallest, Nominal, and Largest Percent Savings 30
3.4. Relative Savings for Drivers Who Retain a Modified Version of Their Current Insurance If Half of Insured Drivers Switch to ANF: Smallest, Nominal, and Largest Percent Savings 31
B.1. Upward Creep of Claimed Economic Loss Distributions: California, 1987 and 1992 42

TABLES

2.1. Compensation Sources for Accident Victims Under the Current System 11
2.2. Compensation Sources for Accident Victims Under the Choice System 14
3.1. Relative Savings for Previously Insured Drivers 19
3.2. Relative Savings Under Choice by State: Tort States 21
3.3. Relative Savings Under Choice by State: No-Fault States 22
3.4. Relative Savings for All Coverages for Insured Switchers Under Different Assumptions 27
3.5. Relative Savings for Insured Switchers Under Different Cost Estimates 28
A.1. Distribution of Accident Victims 37
A.2. Distribution of BI Claims 38
A.3. Distribution of MP (PIP) Claims 39
A.4. Distribution of Claims Under the Current System 39
B.1. Hypothetical Examples of Compensation Under the Current and Proposed Plans 42

SUMMARY

No-fault automobile insurance plans offer cost savings and speedier, more certain compensation to auto accident victims. But, for motorists to obtain those benefits, the state must deny them traditional tort rights unless the costs or nature of their injuries exceeds a specified threshold. Many states confronted with this tradeoff have been unwilling to impose no-fault.

Choice auto insurance was proposed as a response to this policy concern. Under a choice auto insurance system, drivers elect to be insured under either a somewhat modified version of their state's current auto insurance plan or a no-fault plan. In general, the no-fault option under the choice plan could include a tort threshold. We examine a particular choice plan in which the no-fault option is absolute no-fault (ANF). Those who choose ANF are compensated for their economic losses—medical costs, lost wages, burial expenses, the costs of replacement service, and other pecuniary expenditures—up to the policy limit, by their own insurer. They neither recover for nor are liable to others for noneconomic losses—physical and emotional pain and suffering, physical impairment, mental anguish, disfigurement, and other nonpecuniary losses.

Each state's current rules govern the compensation of accident victims covered by the modified current system if they are injured by an uninsured driver or by a driver who elected the modified current system. Accident victims who elected the modified current system and are injured by a driver who elected ANF can recover for both economic and noneconomic losses, to the degree that that driver was responsible for the accident, under applicable state law (e.g., subject to the tort threshold in a current no-fault state). However, compensation would be paid to victims by their own insurer, instead of the ANF driver's insurer. Their recovery would be limited by the limits on a policy they purchased from their insurer, rather than by the limits on the policy the ANF driver purchased (as would be the case under the current system). Any accident victim, regardless of insurance status, may claim against others involved in the accident, based on fault, for uncompensated economic loss. The plan does not affect existing insurance coverage for property damage resulting from auto accidents.

In an earlier study, we estimated the effects of a choice automobile insurance plan on the costs of compensating auto accident victims in which the no-fault option was ANF. We assumed that 50 percent of the consumers who would have purchased auto insurance under their state's current system would switch to ANF under the choice plan. At the request of the Joint Economic Committee of the United States Congress, we next used our data and models to estimate how a variant of that plan would affect the costs of private passenger automobile insurance if all currently insured drivers elected the no-fault option. The data we used in these previous studies described the compensation provided to a representative sample of auto accident victims in 1987.

We have recently obtained comparable data for a representative sample of people who were compensated for auto accident injuries in 1992. Using these more recent data, we replicated our analyses for 46 states. Data limitations forced us to exclude Connecticut, Georgia, Hawaii, and New Jersey in this analysis.

APPROACH

For each state, we estimate the average costs auto insurers incur in compensating a representative sample of accident victims under the current system. We then estimate the average costs insurers would incur under the choice plan for those same accident victims on behalf of either drivers who opt for the modified version of the current system or drivers who elect absolute no-fault. We compare average costs per insured driver under the current system to average costs for drivers who elect either the modified current system or absolute no-fault under the choice plan to determine how the adoption of the choice plan would affect auto insurance costs for drivers who elect either type of insurance.

Our data were collected in 1992; thus, our results pertain to the auto insurance system then in place in each state. Because we focus on the relative costs of absolute no-fault and the modified version of the current system in each state, any factors that proportionately affect costs under both the current system and the choice plan net out in the comparison. Our results are insensitive to changes in such factors over time.

RESULTS

Our analyses of the 1992 data suggest that the choice plan could substantially reduce the costs insurers incur in compensating people injured in automobile accidents. If insurance premiums vary with insurers' costs, drivers in most states who opt for ANF could buy personal injury coverages for about 45 percent, on average, of what they would pay for those coverages under the their state's current auto insurance system. Because personal injury coverages account for a little less than half of total auto insurance premiums (property damage coverages account for just over half of auto insurance premiums), this reduction translates roughly into a 21 percent reduction in the average policyholder's total auto insurance premium. The estimated savings are not very sensitive to the fraction of drivers who elect ANF. These estimates are overall averages: Individual policyholders would realize greater or smaller savings, depending on risk factors such as their driving record and where their car is garaged and on the personal injury and property damage coverages and policy limits they would purchase if ANF were not an option.

At the same time, the plan would have little effect on the costs insurers incur in compensating accident victims covered under the modified version of their state's current system. There is no reason to expect any significant change in the insurance premiums charged policyholders who elect their state's modified current system.

The estimated savings result from reductions in the average amounts insurers pay out in compensation and transaction costs. We estimate that if half of the insured drivers in a state elect ANF, the compensation paid the average insured accident victim for economic losses would be slightly increased: Accident victims covered by the no-fault option are compensated for their economic loss without regard to fault; thus, negligent victims covered by the no-fault option receive greater compensation for economic loss than they would in the current system. Accident victims covered by the modified version of their state's current system generally receive about the same compensation for economic loss as they would have under the current system. The amount of compensation paid to insured victims for noneconomic loss would be cut to the extent that consumers switch to ANF. Victims covered by the modified current system under choice would receive about the same amount of compensation for noneconomic loss as under the current system, assuming that, on average, they purchase coverage limits similar to those purchased now. Those who are covered by ANF would receive no compensation for noneconomic loss. If half of the insured drivers under the current system elect the modified current system and half switch to ANF, the amount paid to insured victims in compensation for noneconomic loss would be reduced a little less than half. There are differences from one victim to another in how the compensation paid to them for economic loss under the choice plan would compare with the compensation they would each have received under the current system.

Insurers' claims handling and defense costs would be reduced about one-sixth, on average. In addition, the choice plan would cut the costs of compensating uninsured motorists.

SENSITIVITY ANALYSIS

We examined the sensitivity of our results to four fundamental assumptions that underlie the analysis—the fraction of drivers who would go uninsured under the current system, the fraction of insured drivers under the current system who would switch to ANF under choice, the fraction of uninsured drivers under the current system who would purchase insurance under choice, and the frequency of very large loss cases. We varied one or another of the assumptions and repeated the entire analysis until we had systematically considered all reasonable possibilities in each state. In all, we developed 81 estimates of the effects of the choice plan on insured switchers' total auto insurance premiums in each state. For most states, the range of estimates is relatively small. Nothing in these estimates poses a serious threat to our main finding that the costs of insuring drivers who elect ANF under choice for personal injury coverages would be reduced about 45 percent, on average, which, if passed on to consumers, would translate into average savings of about 21 percent on total premiums.

For each state, we used the same approach to develop 81 estimates of the effects of the choice plan on total auto insurance premiums to insured stayers—drivers who elect to remain under the modified version of their state's current system. Here, too, the range of estimates is relatively small in most states. Nothing in these estimates poses a serious threat to our main finding—that insured drivers who elect their state's modified current system under choice would not be noticeably affected by the availability of ANF.

WHY THE 1992 RESULTS DIFFER FROM THE 1987 RESULTS

Our updated estimates of the savings under the choice plan are lower than our original estimates, based on the 1987 data. The accident victims in our 1992 database claimed economic losses that were much greater, on average, than the losses claimed by the accident victims in our 1987 database. Because accident victims covered by the no-fault option are compensated for their economic loss without regard for fault, negligent victims covered by the no-fault option receive greater compensation for economic loss than they would under the current system. The growth in average economic losses increased the costs of compensating negligent victims covered by no-fault for their economic losses. At the same time, drivers have generally not increased their policy limits to keep pace with the rate of growth in claimed losses. As a greater fraction of 1992 accident victims' economic loss claims neared insurance policy limits, compensation for noneconomic loss was "squeezed." Consequently, the plan saves less, relative to the current system, with respect to victims who would have been compensated for noneconomic loss under the current system.

ACKNOWLEDGMENTS

We owe thanks to many people for the enormous amount of help that we received. We are particularly indebted to RAND colleagues Lloyd Dixon, Deborah Hensler, Mark Peterson, and Daniel Relles who reviewed earlier drafts of this report and offered numerous helpful comments. We are greatly indebted to Jeffrey O'Connell (University of Virginia) who brought the choice approach to automobile insurance to our attention. We have also benefited from comments and suggestions offered by the members of the ICJ's Board of Overseers who also reviewed both the earlier studies and earlier drafts of this report

A great many people have contributed to our understanding of the workings of auto insurance systems. We cannot name every person who spent time with us; the list would be very long, and several of our conversations were on a nonattribution basis. We generally thank those public officials from many states, including judges, legislative staff, and staff from state insurance departments, who helped us understand the dimensions of the auto insurance policy debate. We also thank the many representatives of private organizations—consumer groups, insurance companies, and the plaintiffs' bar—who shared their perspectives and concerns with us. And we thank the people involved in the day-to-day operations of auto insurance systems—plaintiffs' attorneys, defendants' attorneys, and claims' agents—who devoted many hours of their time to helping us understand how the auto insurance system works in practice.

We used data provided by several organizations. We are particularly indebted to the Insurance Research Council. Much of our analysis is based on the council's Closed Claim and Consumer Panel databases.

Finally, we thank Elizabeth Giddens for helping us structure the report, and Tracy Jenkins for typing the drafts of this report.

ACRONYMS

ANF	Absolute No-Fault plan
BI	Bodily Injury
FR	Financial Responsibility
ICJ	Institute for Civil Justice
IRC	Insurance Research Council
ISO	Insurance Services Office
MP	Medical Payment
NAIC	National Association of Insurance Commissioners
PIP	Personal Injury Protection
PPI	Personal Protection Insurance
TM	Tort Maintenance
UIM	Underinsured Motorist
UM	Uninsured Motorist
XEL	Excess Economic Loss

1. INTRODUCTION

PURPOSES AND SCOPE OF THIS STUDY

In an earlier study, we estimated the effects of a choice automobile insurance plan on the costs of compensating auto accident victims, assuming that 50 percent of the drivers who would purchase insurance under the current system and 50 percent of the drivers who would go uninsured under the current system would elect the no-fault option provided under the choice plan.[1] At the request of the Joint Economic Committee of the United States Congress, we used our data and models to estimate how a variant of that plan would affect the costs of private passenger automobile insurance if all currently insured drivers elected the no-fault option.[2] The data we used in these studies described the compensation provided to a representative sample of auto accident victims in 1987. Recently, we obtained comparable data for a representative sample of people who were compensated for auto accident injuries in 1992. Using these more recent data, we replicated the earlier analyses. Our analyses of the 1992 data suggest that the choice plan could result in substantial savings on auto insurance costs.

The remainder of this section briefly reviews the choice auto insurance plan we examined, summarizes our research approach and the scope and limitations of this analysis, and presents our key findings.

THE CHOICE PLAN

O'Connell et al. (1993) proposed a choice plan for the states in which the traditional tort system governs compensation for auto accident victims. O'Connell et al. (1996) extended the concept to the no-fault states. In 1997, bills that would establish a choice plan in all states were introduced in both the U.S. Senate (S. 626) and the U.S. House of Representatives (HR 2021).[3] Although these plans differ in important details, they all embody the same basic concept: Auto insurance consumers are given a choice between a modified version of their state's current insurance plan and an absolute no-fault (ANF) plan. Those who elect the modified current system can claim for injury based on fault for economic and noneconomic losses under applicable state law to the limits of relevant insurance coverage, which they purchase themselves. Those who elect ANF can claim for injury without regard to fault for economic losses under applicable state law to the limits of relevant

---

[1]Abrahamse and Carroll (1995) provide a detailed description of the methods we used to analyze the effects of the plan.

[2]See Abrahamse and Carroll (1997). The Joint Economic Committee was considering an automobile insurance plan that would include both private passenger and commercial vehicles. Because of data limitations, our analysis was limited to the effects of the plan on private passenger auto insurance and did not consider the plan's effects on the costs of commercial auto insurance.

[3]Both the Senate and House bills would permit a state to opt out of the choice plan and retain its current system.

insurance coverage. Any victim can claim in fault for uncompensated economic loss against a driver who injured them.

For purposes of this analysis, we defined a basic choice plan that incorporates the fundamental concept underlying these various proposals. In the plan we examine here, consumers who opt for the modified current system in the tort states are required to purchase bodily injury (BI) coverage to at least the state's financial responsibility level.[4] They are also required to purchase a new form of insurance, tort maintenance (TM), to at least that level.[5] They may purchase the same optional coverages—medical payments (MP), personal injury protection (PIP), uninsured motorist (UM), and underinsured motorist (UIM)[6]—available in the current system. Consumers who opt for ANF are required to purchase personal protection insurance (PPI) coverage to at least the state's financial responsibility level.[7] They are also required to purchase BI coverage to at least the state's financial responsibility level.[8]

The rules of a state's current system generally govern the amount that auto accident victims who elected the modified current system can recover. If they were entirely at fault for the accident in which they were injured, their recovery is limited to their own MP or PIP coverage. If another driver was at least partially at fault for the accident, they can claim for injury based on fault for economic and noneconomic loss under applicable state law. The choice plan does modify the determination of which insurance coverage is responsible for payment of the claim:

- If injured by a driver who also elected the modified current system, a victim may seek compensation from that driver's insurer to the limits of the BI coverage that driver purchased.

---

[4]BI coverage compensates some other person who sustains injuries for which the insured—the policyholder—is legally responsible. BI compensates the injured party for both economic and noneconomic losses to the extent that the insured was responsible for the injury, up to the BI policy limit.

[5]Tort maintenance coverage compensates the policyholder if he or she is injured by a driver who opted for ANF for both economic and noneconomic losses to the extent that the other driver was responsible for the injury, up to the TM policy limit.

[6]MP covers the insured's own medical expenses (and funeral costs), regardless of fault. It does not cover other economic losses, such as lost earnings, or noneconomic losses, such as pain and suffering. UM compensates the policyholder if he or she is injured by an uninsured motorist for both economic and noneconomic losses to the extent that the other driver was responsible for the injury, up to the UM policy limit. UIM compensates the policyholder for injuries negligently caused by another driver when applicable policy limits (either the other driver's BI limits or the insured's UM limits) constrain the policyholder's recovery, up to the UIM policy limit.

[7]PPI covers the insured's economic losses (and funeral costs), regardless of fault, to the policy limits. It provides essentially the same coverage as the PIP insurance now required in current no-fault systems and available in many of the current tort states. We use the term personal protection insurance in reference to the coverage purchased by consumers who opt for ANF under choice. We use the term personal injury protection in reference to the coverage purchased by consumers who opt for the modified current system under choice in a no-fault state.

[8]This provision departs from the original O'Connell et al. (1993) proposal, which did not require that drivers who opted for ANF purchase supplementary bodily injury coverage.

- If injured by an uninsured driver, a victim may seek compensation from his or her own insurer under his or her UM coverage to the limits purchased.
- If injured by a driver who elected ANF, a victim may seek compensation from his or her own insurer under his or her TM coverage to the limits purchased. A victim may also seek compensation from the other driver's insurer under the other driver's BI coverage for any uncompensated economic loss.

Consumers in the current no-fault states are offered a choice between a modified version of their state's current no-fault plan and ANF. Those who opt for the modified current system in the no-fault states are required to purchase the PIP insurance now required under their state's current system and BI coverage to at least the state's financial responsibility level. They are also required to purchase TM to at least the state's financial responsibility level. They may purchase the same optional coverages available in the current system. Drivers who opt for ANF are required to purchase PPI coverage to at least the level of the PIP insurance now required in their state's current system and BI coverage to at least the state's financial responsibility level.

In a no-fault state, insured victims who elected the modified current system would be compensated for their economic loss by their own PIP coverage up to the policy limit. If another driver was at least partially at fault for the accident and their injuries surmount the tort threshold, they can claim for injury based on fault for economic and noneconomic loss under applicable state law. The choice plan does modify the determination of which insurance coverage is responsible for payment of the claim. Victims injured by a driver who also elected the modified current system may seek compensation from that driver's insurer to the limits of the BI coverage that driver purchased. Victims injured by an uninsured driver may seek compensation from their own insurer under their UM coverage to the limits they purchased. Victims injured by a driver who elected ANF may seek compensation from their own insurer under their TM coverage to the limits they purchased. They may also seek compensation from the other driver's insurer under the other driver's BI coverage for any uncompensated economic loss.

In any state, auto accident victims who elected ANF are compensated by their PPI insurance for any economic losses resulting from the accident, including accidents involving drivers who elected their state's modified current system, without regard for fault, to the PPI policy limit. Drivers electing ANF can never seek compensation for noneconomic losses.[9]

Uninsured drivers injured in auto accidents proceed as under their state's current system if injured by a driver who elected the modified current system or by another uninsured driver. Uninsured drivers injured by another driver who elected ANF can seek

[9]Both the O'Connell et al. (1993, 1996) proposals and the variants proposed in the Senate and House bills would allow an accident victim to recover under tort when the injury was caused by a tortfeasor's alcohol or drug abuse. And ANF electees injured while under the influence of alcohol or illegal drugs would forfeit their PPI benefits. Because of data limitations, we do not consider these provisions in this analysis.

compensation from the other driver for economic losses in excess of the mandated PPI limit, to the extent the other driver was responsible for the accident.

Compensation for injured nondrivers—passengers, pedestrians, bicyclists, and so on—who have purchased auto insurance is governed by the rules relevant to their insurance, even though they were not driving when injured.[10] Compensation for injured nondrivers who have not purchased auto insurance is governed by the rules relevant to the insurance purchased by the driver who injured them.

All drivers, whether they elected the modified current system or ANF, are liable in tort to someone they injure, for economic losses in excess of the mandated TM (if the victim elected the modified current system) or PPI (if the victim elected ANF) coverage. All victims, whether they elected the modified current system or ANF or choose to go uninsured, may seek compensation from someone who injured them for economic losses in excess of the mandated TM (modified current system electees) or PPI (ANF electees) coverage. When claims for excess economic loss are pursued, a reasonable attorney's fee is recoverable, in addition to the excess economic loss.

KEY FINDINGS

Our results suggest that the choice plan could dramatically reduce the costs that insurers incur in compensating people injured in automobile accidents. If insurance premiums are proportional to compensation costs, drivers in most states who opt for ANF could buy personal injury coverages for about 45 percent less, on average, of what they pay for those coverages under their state's current auto insurance system.[11] Because personal injury coverages account for a little less than half of total auto insurance premiums (property damage coverages account for just over half of auto insurance premiums), this reduction translates roughly into a 21 percent reduction in the average policyholder's total auto insurance premium. The estimated savings are not very sensitive to the fraction of drivers who elect ANF. These estimates are overall averages: Individual policyholders would realize greater or smaller savings, depending on risk factors such as their driving record and where their car is garaged as well as on the personal injury and property damage coverages and policy limits they would purchase if ANF were not an option.

At the same time, the plan will have little effect on the costs insurers incur in compensating accident victims covered under the modified version of their state's current system. There is no reason to expect any significant change in the insurance premiums charged policyholders who elect the modified version of their state's current system.

These savings result from reductions in the average amounts insurers pay out in compensation and transaction costs. We estimate that, on average, if half of the insured drivers in a state switched to ANF under choice, the amount paid to insured accident victims

---

[10]Motorists who choose either the current system or ANF bind their resident relatives to that choice.

[11]Our earlier study reported greater savings. Our analysis of the 1987 database suggested that the plan would reduce compensation costs about 60 percent, translating roughly into a 30 percent reduction in premiums.

for economic loss would be increased about 11 percent while the amount paid to them for noneconomic losses would be cut in half. There are differences from one victim to another in how the compensation paid to them for economic loss under the choice plan would compare with the compensation they would each have received under the current system. Insurers' claims handling and defense costs on behalf of insured drivers would be reduced about 15 percent, on average. If half of the victims who would have been uninsured under the current system elect ANF when given the choice, the compensation paid to them would be reduced about 12 percent while the compensation paid to drivers who remain uninsured would be cut 42 percent.

SCOPE AND LIMITATIONS

In this report, we estimate the future costs of compensating a representative sample of private passenger auto accident victims in each state under either its current insurance system or the choice plan described above. The ratio of these estimates indicates the relative costs of compensating the same victims, for the same injuries and losses, under the two plans.[12] Because any factors that proportionately affect costs under both the current system and the choice plan net out in the comparison, the results are insensitive to changes in such factors over time. However, because our results address relative costs, they do not address whether auto insurance costs will rise or fall if a state adopts the choice plan. Rather, they show the difference between what would happen in that state if the current system is retained and what would occur instead if the choice plan were adopted.

We focus on the effects of the choice plan on the costs of private passenger auto insurance. We do not consider the effects of the plan on commercial auto insurance.

We focus on how the choice plan affects auto insurers' compensation costs, including both the amounts insurers pay out in compensation and the transaction costs they incur in providing that compensation.[13] Because the choice plan has no effect on property damage coverages, we do not consider property damage in any of our estimates. To translate our estimates of the effects of the plan on compensation costs into estimates of the effects of the plan on insurance premiums, we assume that the many other factors (e.g., insurers' overhead, profit margins, and investment income) that play a role in determining insurance premiums all vary in proportion to premiums. That is, we estimate savings on compensation costs and then estimate how total premiums would have to vary to maintain the existing ratio of total premiums to compensation costs.

We do not attempt to estimate the plan's effects on the costs of any particular coverage. Specifically, we compare the *average* amount insurers pay per insured driver under all coverages in the current system to the *average* amount paid under all coverages on

[12]We include all accident victims—insured and uninsured drivers, passengers, pedestrians, bicyclists, people injured in single-car accidents, etc.—in these calculations.

[13]Under the choice plan, claimants may recover reasonable attorney's fees for a claim for excess economic loss. The attorney's fees paid by insurers as a result of such claims are included in our estimates.

behalf of drivers who choose either the modified current system or ANF under the choice plan.

It is important for readers to be aware that our estimates reflect the effects of a *basic* choice plan on auto insurance costs and compensation, not the effects of a particular choice proposal. Each choice proposal that has been made to date—the O'Connell et al. plans, S. 625, and HR 2021—includes additional provisions not reflected in this analysis. In particular, each of those proposals would make auto insurance secondary to some other forms of insurance. Under the O'Connell et al. proposals, PPI coverage would be in excess of all collateral sources. The Senate and House bills would make PPI benefits secondary to state mandated workers' compensation and nonoccupational disability benefits. Because our data do not indicate the availability of benefits from collateral sources, we do not consider the effects of these provisions in the analysis. We assume that auto insurance is primary in this analysis.

For each state, we assume that the distribution of TM policy limits purchased by consumers who opt for the modified current system under choice would be the same as the distribution of BI policy limits purchased by consumers under the current system. The compensation for noneconomic loss available to accident victims injured by a driver insured under the current system in each state is limited to that driver's BI policy limits. The compensation for noneconomic loss available to accident victims who elect the modified current system under choice in each state is limited to the victim's TM policy limits. Consequently, our assumption holds constant the average compensation for noneconomic loss available to consumers who elect the modified current system. If consumers who elect the modified current system under choice buy higher TM policy limits, on average, than the BI policy limits purchased under the current system, their savings would be lower, and their access to compensation for noneconomic loss greater, on average, than our estimates. Conversely, if they buy lower TM policy limits, on average, than the BI policy limits purchased under the current system, their savings would be greater, and their access to compensation for noneconomic loss less, on average, than our estimates.

Furthermore, because our focus is on the financial implications of the choice plan, we do not consider the degree to which accident victims derive satisfaction from being compensated under an insurance policy purchased by the driver who injured them.[14] Nor do we consider the satisfaction that consumers who value access to compensation for noneconomic loss derive from being able to determine for themselves the limits on what they can obtain if injured by another driver in an auto accident rather than facing the uncertainty of the policy limit purchased by that driver.

The current system in most states encourages excess claiming as a means of leveraging larger settlements from auto insurers.[15] The ANF option would eliminate this incentive for excess claims. To the extent that the distributions of claimed economic losses reflect excess claiming in response to the current system, drivers who elect ANF under choice

[14]See Hensler et al. (1991), Section V, for a review of the literature on the factors that motivate claiming.

[15]See, for example, Carroll et al. (1995) or Insurance Research Council (September 1994).

would submit fewer, smaller claims than we assume. The choice plan might result in greater savings than those reported here.

We had to exclude Connecticut, Georgia, Hawaii, and New Jersey from this analysis because of data limitations. The data used here were collected in 1992. Connecticut, in 1993, and Hawaii, in 1998, subsequently changed their auto insurance system; accordingly, our data do not provide a basis for estimating the effects of shifting from the current plan to a choice plan in either state. Georgia repealed its no-fault law in 1991. Our data for Georgia include both claims filed under the earlier no-fault regime and claims filed under the current tort regime, and we cannot determine which regime affected any particular claim. Here, too, our data do not allow us to estimate how adoption of a choice plan would affect insurance costs in Georgia. Finally, because of a misunderstanding when the data were collected, the New Jersey data available to us may not be representative of the distribution of auto insurance claims in that state.

In 1992, Pennsylvania offered consumers a choice plan under which they could elect either tort or a verbal threshold no-fault plan.[16] We performed separate analyses for the effects of each plan. In the subsequent tables, the effects of the plan on Pennsylvania drivers who elected tort, labeled Penn (tort), are included in the results for the tort states; the effects of the plan on Pennsylvania drivers who elected no-fault (labeled Penn nof in the following figures), are included in the results for the no-fault states.

ORGANIZATION OF THE DISCUSSION

The remainder of this discussion is organized as follows. In Section 2, we describe our research approach, including the data and the methods we used to estimate compensation costs under either the current system or the choice plan in each state and the relative savings under the choice plan compared to the current system. Section 3 presents our findings and describes the sensitivity analyses we conducted. Finally, Section 4 contains our conclusions. Appendix A presents the technical details of certain calculations. Appendix B discusses the differences between the estimates presented here and those we reported earlier.

---

[16]Under a verbal threshold auto insurance plan, injured parties may seek compensation for noneconomic loss if they have suffered certain injuries specified in the law. Examples of the language found in the various verbal thresholds now in use are "death" (all), "significant and permanent loss of an important bodily function" (Florida), "permanent serious disfigurement" (Michigan and Pennsylvania), "dismemberment" (New Jersey), and "permanent consequential limitation of use of a body function or system" (New York).

2. RESEARCH APPROACH

We estimate the relative cost effects of the choice plan in each state in three steps: (1) We estimate the average cost of compensating accident victims under the current system and the corresponding "break-even premium"—the premium an insurance company must charge to cover exactly what it pays in claims and the associated transaction costs; (2) we estimate the average cost of compensating accident victims on behalf of drivers who elect either the modified current system or ANF under the choice system and the "break-even premiums" for each class of driver; and (3) we calculate relative savings under choice as the percentage difference between the break-even premium under choice for drivers who elect either option and the break-even premium under the current system.

We describe our data and each of these steps below. We use California to illustrate our methodology.

DATA

The analysis relies on data from four sources: closed claim surveys conducted by the Insurance Research Council (IRC);[1] a consumer panel study, also conducted by IRC;[2] special tabulations compiled at our request by the Insurance Services Office (ISO); and National Association of Insurance Commissioners (NAIC) reports on auto insurance premiums by type of coverage.[3]

The closed claim surveys obtained detailed information on a national representative sample of auto accident injury claims closed with payment during 1992 under each of the principal auto injury coverages—BI, MP, UM, UIM, and PIP.[4] The data detail each victim's accident and resulting injuries and losses, as well as the compensation each claimant obtained from auto insurance. The data were collected by 61 insurance companies that, together, accounted for about 72 percent of private passenger automobile insurance by premium volume at the time the data were collected. In each state and for each coverage, the survey represents a simple random sample of all claims closed in that state by the participating companies.[5]

---

[1]Insurance Research Council (September 1994) provides a detailed description of the closed claim surveys.

[2]Insurance Research Council (May 1994) provides a detailed description of the consumer panel survey.

[3]National Association of Insurance Commissioners (1997).

[4]These are the most recent available data that describe the outcomes of a national sample of individual claims.

[5]The sampling fraction differs from state to state. We estimate the effects of the choice plan in each state, using the data for that state. To obtain an estimate of the nationwide effects of the plan, we combine the results across states, weighting the result for each state by the product of the sampling fraction for that state and the number of auto insurance policies sold in that state in 1992. We obtained the data on the number of policies written in each state from National Association of Insurance Commissioners (1997).

The IRC consumer panel survey contains data on the experiences of households in which someone was injured in an auto accident between 1989 and 1991. A total of 180,000 households in a national panel maintained by National Family Opinion, Inc., were screened to identify those in which a member had suffered an injury in an auto accident within the previous three years. A follow-up survey of households identified as having been involved in an injury-producing accident obtained detailed information on their compensation experiences. We used the consumer panel survey to estimate the fractions of auto accident victims who obtained compensation from either first- or third-party auto insurance, or both, or who did not receive compensation from any form of auto insurance.

We used the ISO data to estimate insurers' transaction costs,[6] including both allocated loss-adjustment costs—legal fees and related expenses incurred on behalf of and directly attributed to a specific claim—and unallocated, or general claims processing, costs, for each line of private passenger auto insurance.[7] We estimate insurers' allocated loss-adjustment expenses as 1 percent of MP compensation paid, 1 percent of PIP compensation paid, 10 percent of BI compensation paid, and 8 percent of UM or UIM compensation paid. We estimate insurers' unallocated loss-adjustment expenses as 8 percent of paid compensation for each type of coverage. The plan provides that anyone who seeks compensation for economic loss in excess of the mandated PIP limit can recover attorneys' fees; we assume claimants' attorneys' fees average 31 percent.[8]

The NAIC reports private passenger automobile insurance premiums by state and coverage for 1995, the most recent year for which these data are available.

ESTIMATING COMPENSATION COSTS UNDER THE CURRENT SYSTEM

To estimate compensation costs under the current system, we identified the sources of auto insurance compensation that would be available to accident victims, depending on the type of insurance that they, and others, purchase. We then estimated the average amount of compensation that would be paid by each source, and the associated transaction costs, to a representative sample of auto accident victims from each state. Finally, we assumed a distribution of insurance purchase decisions (i.e., the coverages and limits purchased) and computed the expected compensation paid to the average accident victim, given that distribution. The result is an estimate of the compensation costs, including transaction costs, incurred under each state's current system for the assumed distribution of insurance purchase decisions.

---

[6]Carroll et al. (1991), Appendix D, describe the data and methods used to estimate insurers' transaction costs.

[7]We do not include claimants' legal costs, the value of claimants' time, or the costs the courts incur in handling litigated claims. Those costs do not affect insurers' costs and hence do not affect auto insurance premiums.

[8]We do not suggest that attorneys will necessarily charge accident victims a 31 percent contingency fee to represent them in seeking compensation for economic loss in excess of policy limits. However, plaintiff attorneys' fees now average about 31 percent of victims' recovery. If plaintiff attorneys' compensation in the current system is reasonable and fair, their fees, whether charged on an hourly basis, as a contingency, or by some other system, would presumably be approximately as large, relative to the victims' recovery, under the choice plan.

In the sensitivity analyses, discussed in Section 3, we examined the extent to which our estimates vary with alternative compensation estimates or assumed distributions of insurance purchase decisions.

Table 2.1 indicates the sources of compensation available to an accident victim under the current system in a tort state, depending on the victim's insurance status, whether another driver was at least partially at fault for the accident,[9] and, if so, whether that driver was insured. The corresponding table for an add-on state[10] in which PIP coverage was available, instead of or in addition to MP coverage, would look exactly the same except that insured accident victims (those in the bottom row) would have access to PIP, if they had purchased that coverage. The corresponding table for a no-fault state would look exactly the same except that insured accident victims (those in the bottom row) would have access to PIP in every case.

Table 2.1

Compensation Sources for Accident Victims Under the Current System

Insurance Status	Other Driver at Least Partially at Fault: Uninsured	Other Driver at Least Partially at Fault: Insured	No Other Driver at Fault
Uninsured victim	0	BI	0
Insured victim	UM	MP + BI	MP

To estimate compensation costs for each state, we use our data on the compensation given to a representative sample of accident victims and the associated transaction costs, as follows.

UNINSURED ACCIDENT VICTIMS

We assume that an uninsured accident victim injured either in an accident caused by a driver who is also uninsured or in an accident in which no other driver is at least partially at fault receives no compensation from auto insurance.

We estimate the costs of compensating an uninsured accident victim injured in an accident with an insured, at-fault driver as the average compensation paid on BI claims ($8,435 in California) times the probability that an accident victim exceeds the tort

[9]In our earlier studies, we assumed that all victims injured in multicar accidents had access to another driver's third-party coverage with the probability that the other driver was insured. In this study, we assume that victims who were injured in accidents in which no other driver was at least partially at fault have access only to their own first-party coverage, regardless of the number of cars involved in the accident. Specifically, we assume, using IRC data, that 30 percent of victims were injured in accidents in which no other driver was at least partially at fault. Section 3 presents tests of the sensitivity of the results to alternative assumptions regarding the percentage.

[10]Add-on states are those in which PIP coverage is available, but there is no tort threshold.

threshold.[11] We assume that average transaction costs are 18 percent of BI compensation in all states.

INSURED ACCIDENT VICTIMS

We estimate the costs in tort states of compensating an insured accident victim injured in an accident caused by an uninsured driver as the average compensation paid on UM claims ($7,167 in California) times the fraction of insured drivers in the state who purchased UM coverage (0.89).[12]

In the no-fault states, we assume compensation costs as the average compensation paid on PIP claims, plus the average compensation paid on UM claims times the fraction of insured drivers in the state who purchased UM coverage times the probability that an accident victim exceeds the tort threshold. We assume that average transaction costs are 9 percent of PIP compensation paid and 18 percent of UM compensation paid.

We estimate the costs of compensating an insured accident victim injured in an accident with another insured driver in a tort (no-fault) state as the sum of the average compensation paid on BI claims in that state plus transaction costs ($9,953 in California) plus the average compensation paid on MP (PIP) claims in that state plus transaction costs ($2,886 in California) times the probability that the victim will claim against both his or her own first-party and the other driver's third-party coverages. We use the ratio of MP-earned exposures to BI-earned exposures in each state as our estimate of the fraction of insured accident victims who have access to MP coverage.[13] We use the consumer panel survey data to estimate the probability that a victim with access to MP coverage will pursue a claim against that coverage.[14]

We assume that all insured accident victims in the no-fault states have PIP coverage and will seek compensation under that coverage. We assume that transaction costs are 9 percent of MP or PIP compensation paid and 18 percent of BI compensation paid.

We estimate the costs of compensating an insured accident victim injured in an accident in which no other driver was at fault in tort (no-fault) states as the average compensation paid on MP (PIP) claims times the fraction of insured drivers in the state who

---

[11]By definition, all accident victims "exceed the tort threshold" in tort states. In a no-fault state, we take the fraction of PIP claims that the claims' adjuster judged qualified for a BI tort recovery under the no-fault law, whether or not the claimant actually pursued a tort claim.

[12]We use the ratio of UM-earned exposures to BI-earned exposures in each state as our estimate of the fraction of insured accident victims who have UM coverage. The National Association of Independent Insurers (1995) reports earned exposures by coverage for each state except Massachusetts, North Carolina, South Carolina, and Texas. We use the national average ratio of exposures for these states.

[13]National Association of Independent Insurers (1995).

[14]In our earlier studies, we assumed that any victim with access to both first- and third-party compensation would seek both. In this study, we assume, using IRC data, that 50 percent of victims with access to both first- and third-party compensation get both while the other 50 percent get only their own, first-party compensation. For all practical purposes, we changed a number we use in making various calculations from 1.0 to 0.5. Section 4 presents tests of the sensitivity of the results to alternative assumptions regarding the percentage.

purchased MP (PIP) coverage. We assume that transaction costs are 9 percent of MP or PIP compensation paid.

ESTIMATING THE DISTRIBUTION OF ACCIDENT VICTIMS

The IRC consumer panel study data indicate the fractions of auto accident victims who are compensated by their own or another's auto insurance. For example, in California, auto accident victims reported compensation from auto insurance as follows:

- Only own auto insurance: 27 percent,
- Only another driver's auto insurance: 36 percent,
- Both own and another driver's auto insurance: 21 percent, and
- No compensation from any auto insurer: 16 percent.

The last category includes both accident victims who had no access to any form of auto insurance (e.g., an uninsured victim injured by an uninsured driver or who was entirely responsible for the accident) and victims who chose not to pursue an available claim (e.g., an accident victim who was compensated by some source other than auto insurance, such as their own health insurance, and chose not to bring a claim against his or her own or another's auto insurance policy). Given an estimate of the uninsured motorist rate, these results are sufficient to estimate the distribution of accident victims among the cells in Table 2.1.[15]

Because state-specific estimates of uninsured motorist rates are not readily available, we take a parametric approach: We assume that the uninsured motorist rate is 15 percent.[16] We then compute the resulting fraction of accident victims that would be found in each cell of Table 2.1, multiply that fraction by the corresponding compensation costs, and sum over the cells. The result is an estimate of the average cost of compensating an accident victim in each state under that state's current system. The product of this estimate and the ratio of accident victims to insured drivers in that state is the amount that the state's insured drivers would have to be charged, on average, to recover the costs of compensating all victims. We then vary the assumed uninsured motorist rate and repeat the procedure. Section 3 describes the sensitivity of the results to the assumed uninsured motorist rate.

In California, for example, if 15 percent of drivers are uninsured, the average cost of compensating auto accident victims under the current system will be $7,894. To break even, insurers would have to charge the average insured driver $9,288 * V, where V is the ratio of accident victims to insured drivers. We lack data on V for each state. However, we show later that this number cancels out when we compute the ratio of costs under the current system to costs under the choice system in a given state.

---

[15]Appendix A details the calculations.

[16]Using the ratio of UM to BI claim frequencies to estimate the uninsured motorist rate, the All-Industry Research Advisory Council (now the Insurance Research Council) (1989) estimated that about 13 percent of drivers were uninsured in the mid-1980s. Miller, Rapp, Herbers, & Terry, Inc., an actuarial consulting firm, estimated the frequencies of UM and BI claims in the tort states in the early 1990s. The ratio of their estimates is about 0.15 (private communication).

Note that under the assumption that insurance purchase decisions are statistically independent of subsequent accidents and the resulting injuries and losses, the estimates we obtain for each state are identical to those we would have obtained by estimating expected compensation outcomes for each individual victim and averaging over the victims in the sample for each state. In other words, the method outlined above essentially takes account of the variations in relevant accident characteristics (e.g., the victim's negligence) and injuries/losses among individual accident victims.

ESTIMATING COMPENSATION COSTS UNDER THE CHOICE SYSTEM

To estimate average compensation costs under the choice system, we made assumptions about drivers' insurance purchase decisions and estimated what insurers' compensation costs will be given those assumptions. In Section 3, we explore the sensitivity of our results to these assumptions and provide estimates of what costs would be under alternative assumptions.

Observe a driver who is uninsured under his state's current system and has declined to purchase the coverage—BI or no-fault—mandated under that system. We assume that, under choice, he would *not* purchase the coverage that he declined before ANF became an option. Thus, under choice, a driver who is uninsured in the current system would either remain uninsured or would opt for ANF under the choice plan. Similarly, a driver who is insured under his state's current system preferred the coverage—BI or no-fault—mandated under that system to going uninsured. Hence, we assume that if a driver *does* have insurance under his or her state's current system, he or she would elect either to retain the modified version of that insurance or to switch to ANF under choice, but would *not* decide to drop automobile insurance coverage altogether.

Given these assumptions, Table 2.2 indicates the sources of compensation available to accident victims in a tort state under the choice plan, depending on their insurance status, whether another driver was at least partially responsible for the accident, and, if so, whether the other driver involved in the accident was insured. The corresponding table for a no-fault state would look exactly the same except that insured accident victims (those in the bottom row) would have access to PIP in every case.

Table 2.2

Compensation Sources for Accident Victims Under the Choice System

Insurance	Other Driver at Least Partially at Fault			No Other
Status	Uninsured	ANF	Current	Driver at Fault
Uninsured victim	0	XEL[a]	BI	0
ANF victim	PPI	PPI + XEL	PPI+ XEL	PPI
Current	UM	TM + XEL	MP + BI	MP

[a]XEL denotes excess economic loss.

In each state, we estimate compensation costs under the choice plan as follows.

ACCIDENTS NOT INVOLVING AN ANF INSURED

The current system's compensation rules govern in accidents that do not involve a victim or driver covered by ANF under choice. We use the methods described above to estimate compensation in these cases.

UNINSURED VICTIMS OF ACCIDENTS CAUSED BY AN ANF INSURED

An uninsured victim injured in an accident involving another car whose driver switched to ANF is compensated by the other driver's supplemental BI insurance for any economic loss in excess of the mandated PPI policy limit. We estimate the expected value of compensation for excess economic loss, denoted XEL in Table 2.2, in three steps: First, we compute the difference, if positive, between the victim's economic loss and the mandated PPI limit up to each possible value of the BI policy limit, weighted by the distribution of BI policy limits in the state. We then multiply by one minus the victim's degree of fault for the accident. Finally, we average over all victims in the state. In California, for example, we estimate that compensation for excess economic loss will average $1,300. We assume that transaction costs are 49 percent of compensation paid for excess economic loss—18 percent in insurer's costs and 31 percent in plaintiff's attorney fees.[17] Thus, XEL equals $1,936 in California.

ACCIDENT VICTIMS COVERED BY ANF

We estimate compensation costs for accident victims covered by ANF under choice as their own PPI coverage plus recovery of excess economic loss. We estimate PPI as the average value of victims' economic losses up to the PPI policy limit. We estimate XEL as described above. We assume that transaction costs are 9 percent of PPI compensation and 49 percent of XEL compensation.

VICTIMS COVERED BY THE MODIFIED CURRENT SYSTEM INJURED IN ACCIDENTS CAUSED BY AN ANF INSURED

Victims covered by the modified current system who are injured in an accident caused by a driver who switched to ANF are compensated by their own TM coverage. Because the amount an accident victim can recover under TM is governed by the same rules that govern the amount an insured driver can recover under the state's current system, we estimate average TM compensation costs using the methods described above to estimate BI compensation costs under the current system (e.g., $9,953 in California). Drivers who chose the modified current system are compensated by the other driver's supplemental BI insurance for any economic loss in excess of the TM policy limit. We estimate XEL for victims covered by the modified current system as the difference, if positive, between the victim's economic loss and his or her TM recovery up to each possible value of the BI policy limit, weighted by the distribution of BI policy limits in the state. We then multiply by one minus the victim's degree of fault for the accident. Finally, we average over all victims in the

---

[17]Because the O'Connell et al. (1993) plan provides that victims who seek recovery of excess economic losses may recover their legal costs, we assume that all such victims will seek representation.

state. We assume that transaction costs are 18 percent of TM compensation paid and 49 percent of XEL compensation.

Given the assumed uninsured motorist rate under the current system and the other parameters that describe claiming patterns under the current system, the distribution of accident victims among the cells in Table 2.2 depends on the rate at which drivers who would have been insured under the current system opt for ANF coverage and the rate at which drivers who would have gone uninsured under the current system opt for ANF coverage. We have no data that allow us to estimate what either of these rates would be in any particular state. Accordingly, we take a parametric approach: We assume values for each of these rates, estimate the effects of the choice plan, conditional on those values, and then revise the assumed values and repeat the analysis.

We assume that drivers' insurance purchase decisions are statistically independent of whether or not they will cause, or be injured in, an auto accident. We group drivers into three types according to their insurance purchase decisions and estimate the compensation costs insurers incur on behalf of each type of driver. Specifically, we estimate the costs incurred by insurers under policies purchased by

1. *Stayers*: drivers who would be insured under the current system who select the modified current system under choice,
2. *Insured switchers*: drivers who would be insured under the current system who select ANF under choice, and
3. *Uninsured switchers*: drivers who would be uninsured under the current system who select ANF under choice.

We used the methods discussed above to compute the probability that an accident victim would fall into each cell in Table 2.2. We then multiplied those probabilities by the corresponding compensation costs. The result is an estimate of the average costs insurers incur in compensating a representative sample of accident victims in each state under the choice plan on behalf of drivers who make each possible type of insurance purchase decision. In any state, the estimate for each type of driver, multiplied by the ratio of accident victims paid on behalf of that type of driver to the number of insured drivers of that type, is the average amount insurers would have to charge that type of driver to recover the costs of compensating victims on their behalf. (Recall that we lack data on the number of accident victims per insured driver of each type in each state. As noted above, this number will cancel out when we compute the ratio of compensation costs under the current system to compensation costs under the choice plan for each type of driver.)

Note that, under the assumption that insurance purchase decisions are statistically independent of subsequent accidents and the resulting injuries/losses, the estimates we obtain for each state are identical to those we would have obtained by estimating expected compensation outcomes for each individual victim and averaging over the victims in the sample for each state. In other words, the method outlined above essentially takes account of the variations in relevant accident characteristics (e.g., the victim's negligence) and injuries/losses among individual accident victims.

BREAK-EVEN PERSONAL INJURY PREMIUMS

To calculate the break-even personal injury premium for the current system, assume that there are N drivers, that the average driver is involved in k injury-producing accidents per year, and that each injury costs insurers C dollars, on average, including transaction costs (that is C dollars for *every* injury, including injuries suffered by pedestrians, passengers, bicyclists, and insured and uninsured drivers). Insurers will pay out kNC dollars a year.

Let X denote the fraction of all drivers who are insured. Let P be the average premium that insurers must charge to just cover what they pay out in claims and associated transaction costs. To break even, P must be set such that XNP = kNC. Thus, the break-even premium is P = Ck/X. We know how to calculate C. In calculating relative savings under choice, we will assume the value of X and specify k as an unknown parameter.

RELATIVE SAVINGS ON COMPENSATION COSTS

To calculate *relative* savings on compensation costs, we extended the above notation to three notional insurance companies. The first sells all the insurance policies purchased by drivers in a state under its current system. The second sells all insurance policies purchased by drivers in that state who elect the modified current system under the choice plan. The third sells all insurance policies purchased by drivers in that state who elect ANF under the choice plan. The effects of the choice plan on the costs insurers incur on behalf of drivers who are insured in the traditional system and who would elect the modified current system under choice are reflected in the ratio of the second company's break-even premium to the first company's break-even premium. Similarly, the effects of the choice plan on the costs insurers incur on behalf of drivers who are insured in the current system and who would elect ANF under choice are reflected in the ratio of the third and first companies' break-even premiums.

Assume that the fraction of drivers insured in the current system is X_1 and that the company that insures them pays out an average C_1 dollars for every injury. The corresponding parameters for the company that insures drivers electing the modified current system under choice are X_c and C_c, respectively. The break-even personal injury premium for the current system company is $P_1 = kC_1/X_1$. The break-even personal injury premium for the company that insures modified current system electees under choice is $P_c = kC_c/X_c$. The ratio of the two companies' break-even personal injury premiums is P_c/P_1. The number of injury-producing accidents per driver per year, k, cancels out, and this expression depends only on the fraction insured by each company (the Xs) and the amount of compensation paid for each injury (the Cs).

In California, for example, if 15 percent of drivers are uninsured and half of those who would have been insured under the current system switch to ANF under choice, the average cost of compensating auto accident victims on behalf of insured switchers under the choice plan will be $2,226. To break even, insurers would have to charge the average insured switcher $5,238 * V, where V is the ratio of accident victims to insured drivers. Thus, we estimate that the costs that insurers would incur in compensating auto accident victims on behalf of insured switchers would be about 56 percent ($5,238 / $9,288) of the costs insurers would incur in compensating auto accident victims on behalf of these drivers under the current system. In other words, the costs insurers incur in compensating auto accident victims on behalf of insured switchers under choice would be about 44 percent less than the costs they would have incurred on behalf of those policyholders had choice not been available.

We made a corresponding set of calculations for the ratio of the break-even personal injury premiums for the first and third companies.

In our calculations, we made assumptions about the Xs and estimated the Cs, so we could compare the relative change in the break-even personal injury premium for drivers who elect either their state's modified current system or ANF under choice without knowing the accident rate, assuming that the accident rate remains the same.

RELATIVE SAVINGS ON TOTAL PREMIUMS

The calculations described above yield estimates of the average compensation costs insurers will incur on behalf of stayers, insured switchers, and uninsured switchers under choice, relative to the compensation costs they would have incurred on behalf of each type of driver under their state's current system. To translate the effects on compensation costs under personal injury coverages into effects on total auto insurance premiums, we multiply our estimate of compensation cost savings by the proportion of total auto insurance premiums in each state that were spent for personal injury coverages in 1995, the most recent year for which data are available. In California, for example, total auto insurance premiums added up to almost $12 billion in 1995: about $7.6 billion for liability coverages and about $4.4 billion for collision and comprehensive coverages. Assuming that property damage liability accounted for about 20 percent of liability premiums, drivers spent about $6.1 billion, roughly half the total premium, for personal injury coverages. If insurers' operating costs—overhead, sales expenses, taxes, license fees, etc.—vary in proportion to premiums, a 44 percent reduction in compensation costs would allow insurers to reduce aggregate automobile insurance premiums by about 22 percent and still maintain the same rate of pretax profits on premium income.

3. RESULTS AND SENSITIVITY ANALYSIS

OVERVIEW

We have no data that allow us to estimate the fraction of drivers in each state who would purchase insurance under the current system and would switch to ANF under choice. We consider a nominal case in which we assume that 50 percent of currently insured drivers switch to ANF. In response to the Joint Economic Committee's interest, we also consider the case in which all currently insured drivers elect ANF under choice. The savings realized by currently insured drivers who elect ANF under choice do not depend on the percentage of uninsured drivers who elect ANF under choice. Table 3.1 summarizes the results of the analysis.

We estimate that if half the insured drivers in the *tort states* were to switch to ANF under the choice plan, the costs of compensating victims on their behalf would be reduced about 46 percent from what they would have been had those drivers been insured under the traditional tort system. If insurers' other costs vary in proportion to compensation costs, this would translate into a 20 percent reduction in total auto insurance premiums. Adoption of the choice plan would have little effect on the costs of compensating victims on behalf of drivers who choose to stay under the modified version of the current system.

Averaging over the *no-fault states*, if half the insured drivers were to switch to ANF under the choice plan, the costs of compensating victims on their behalf would be reduced about 45 percent from what the costs would have been had those drivers been insured under their state's current system. If insurers' other costs vary in proportion to compensation costs, this would translate into a 22 percent reduction in total auto insurance premiums. Adoption of the choice plan would reduce the costs of compensating victims on behalf of drivers who elect to remain in the modified current system by about 9 percent, resulting in a 4 percent savings on their total premiums.

Table 3.1

Relative Savings for Previously Insured Drivers (in percent)

			Relative Savings		
Scenario	Insurance Class	Premium	Tort States	No-Fault States	All States
Half switch	Switchers	Personal injury	45.7	44.9	45.3
		Total	20.0	22.1	20.7
	Stayers	Personal injury	1.5	9.2	4.6
		Total	0.9	3.9	1.8
All switch	Switchers	Personal injury	43.8	47.0	45.1
		Total	19.3	23.0	20.5

SOURCE: 1992 data for those compensated for automobile accidents.

Assuming that all insured drivers switch to ANF has little effect on the estimates. In the tort states, compensation costs would be reduced about 44 percent, which translates into a 19 percent reduction in total auto insurance premiums. The corresponding estimates for the no-fault states are a 47 percent reduction in compensation costs and a 23 percent reduction in total auto insurance premiums.

For all states combined, compensation costs incurred on behalf of insured switchers would be reduced about 45 percent. This translates into a 21 percent reduction in total premiums.

These results formally pertain to the situation that existed in each state when our data were collected, in 1992. However, we believe that the results generally describe what would happen in each state if it were to adopt a choice plan at some future date. Because we estimated savings in terms of the ratio of expected compensation costs under choice to expected compensation costs under the current system, our results are insensitive to changes over time in any factors that proportionately affect compensation costs under either plan. Further, in both tort states and no-fault states, differences among states are relatively small. They may reflect sampling errors in our estimates or differences in the extent to which our assumptions apply. In any case, our general results are robust with respect to interstate variations in the distributions of accidents and injuries. This suggests that, even if these distributions vary over time in any state, the variations are not likely to significantly affect our results.

THE EFFECTS OF THE CHOICE PLAN ON COSTS

Tables 3.2 and 3.3 present state-by-state estimates[1] of the average percentage reduction in both personal injury compensation costs and total auto insurance premiums that policyholders who elect either their state's modified current system or ANF would realize in each of the states. These estimates assume that

1. 15 percent of drivers in the state were uninsured under the current system,
2. Either 50 percent or 100 percent of the drivers insured under the current system would opt for ANF if given the choice, and
3. Half of all drivers who were uninsured under the current system would opt for ANF if given the choice.

Drivers who opt for ANF under choice are not liable for others' noneconomic losses. In the tort states, the compensation costs that insurers would incur on behalf of such drivers would be substantially lower than they would have been under the tort system. On the other hand, the amounts paid to them under their PPI coverages generally exceed what would be paid to them under MP insurance. In general, the savings obtained by eliminating

[1]We report the effects of the choice plan on Pennsylvania drivers covered by tort in 1992 in Table 3.2. We report the effects of the choice plan on Pennsylvania drivers covered by the verbal threshold, no-fault plan in 1992 in Table 3.3.

Table 3.2

Relative Savings Under Choice by State: Tort States (in percent)

	Half Switch Scenario				All Switch Scenario	
	Switchers		Stayers		Switchers	
State	Injury Premium	Total Premium	Injury Premium	Total Premium	Injury Premium	Total Premium
Alabama	45.4	15.1	6.0	2.0	43.3	14.4
Alaska	53.7	21.3	6.5	2.6	52.5	20.8
Arizona	47.6	23.7	4.6	2.3	45.3	22.5
Arkansas	61.3	22.5	10.0	3.7	60.4	22.2
California	43.6	19.6	2.9	1.3	42.1	18.9
Delaware	49.6	26.8	–4.7	–2.6	43.7	23.6
Idaho	17.5	7.0	–13.5	–5.4	17.8	7.1
Illinois	39.4	14.6	–2.1	–0.8	37.5	13.9
Indiana	51.8	20.6	2.0	0.8	50.5	20.1
Iowa	67.7	24.4	12.4	4.5	66.5	23.9
Louisiana	62.8	32.5	5.5	2.8	59.7	30.8
Maine	55.9	22.1	1.2	0.5	51.3	20.3
Maryland	52.4	23.5	6.3	2.8	51.6	23.2
Mississippi	48.7	17.2	0.6	0.2	46.2	16.3
Missouri	44.0	16.7	2.9	1.1	43.5	16.4
Montana	59.3	23.5	8.3	3.3	57.2	22.6
Nebraska	37.4	12.9	–4.4	–1.5	35.9	12.3
Nevada	50.8	26.2	2.9	1.5	49.4	25.4
New Hampshire	56.6	22.4	1.4	0.6	52.3	20.7
New Mexico	36.0	16.2	2.5	1.1	34.8	15.7
North Carolina	33.8	16.0	–1.2	–0.6	32.3	15.3
Ohio	48.6	19.4	0.7	0.3	43.5	17.4
Oklahoma	54.4	22.1	1.2	0.5	52.0	21.1
Oregon	47.6	21.8	3.0	1.4	47.5	21.7
Penn Tort	40.4	18.6	0.1	0.1	38.9	17.9
Rhode Island	59.8	30.7	4.3	2.2	57.2	29.4
South Carolina	39.4	17.7	–1.8	–0.8	37.9	17.0
South Dakota	11.1	4.5	–17.0	–6.9	7.7	3.2
Tennessee	47.1	16.5	5.0	1.8	44.8	15.7
Texas	47.9	23.7	5.2	2.6	47.3	23.4
Vermont	29.4	10.8	–16.2	–5.9	26.2	9.6
Virginia	37.6	17.6	–3.9	–1.8	36.6	17.1
Washington	61.6	31.2	5.7	2.9	60.4	30.6
West Virginia	58.3	26.3	7.6	3.4	55.4	25.0
Wisconsin	24.5	9.7	–11.2	–4.4	22.9	9.0
Wyoming	68.9	23.3	7.0	2.4	68.8	23.2
All tort states	45.7	20.0	1.5	0.9	43.8	19.3

SOURCE: 1992 data for those compensated for automobile accidents.

compensation payments on their behalf for noneconomic loss under choice greatly outweigh the additional costs incurred in providing them with more generous first-party no-fault compensation—PPI versus MP. Hence, the cost of compensating for personal injuries incurred or caused by tort state drivers who elect ANF would drop substantially—more than 40 percent in most states—relative to the costs incurred on their behalf under the traditional

Table 3.3

Relative Savings Under Choice by State: No-Fault States (in percent)

	Half Switch Scenario				All Switch Scenario	
	Switchers		Stayers		Switchers	
State	Injury Premium	Total Premium	Injury Premium	Total Premium	Injury Premium	Total Premium
Colorado	49.9	24.0	12.1	5.8	49.7	23.9
Florida	49.2	24.4	7.4	3.7	50.1	24.8
Kansas	25.4	8.2	–6.0	–1.9	27.1	8.7
Kentucky	36.0	15.2	0.5	0.2	37.6	15.9
Massachusetts	59.6	31.0	7.3	3.8	62.7	32.6
Michigan	23.5	10.0	17.1	7.2	29.5	12.5
Minnesota	39.8	19.5	6.9	3.4	38.8	19.1
New York	62.1	28.1	7.9	3.6	62.8	28.5
North Dakota	74.7	24.8	23.9	7.9	75.4	25.0
Penn nof	30.4	14.0	3.8	1.8	35.0	16.2
Utah	60.8	25.8	11.6	4.9	61.1	26.0
All no-fault states	44.9	22.1	9.2	3.9	47.0	23.0

SOURCE: 1992 data for those compensated for automobile accidents.

tort system. If insurers' other costs declined in proportion, the total premiums charged drivers who would be insured under the tort system and would opt for ANF under choice would be reduced by more than 15 percent in most tort states.

The savings that would be realized by insured drivers who switch to ANF under choice are not very sensitive to the fraction of insured drivers who exercise that option. The estimated savings to drivers when 50 percent of insured drivers switch to ANF are very similar to the savings estimates when all insured drivers switch to ANF.[2]

A driver who elected the modified current system and is involved in an accident with a driver who chose ANF is entirely free from liability to the other driver for noneconomic loss; his insurer would pay out less, on average, under choice than under the current system. But a driver who chose the modified current system and is injured in an accident with a driver who chose ANF must turn to his own TM coverage, rather than to the other driver, for recovery of his own noneconomic loss. His insurer saves the costs of compensating the other driver for noneconomic loss but incurs the additional costs of compensating the insured for his own noneconomic loss. If there is no adverse selection in the choices made under the

---

[2]In most of the tort states, the savings available to an individual consumer who switches from the current system to ANF are slightly greater if half of those who would have been insured under the current system switch to ANF than if all of those who would have been insured under the current system switch to ANF. This result stems from the provision that ANF electees are liable to anyone they injure (to the degree they are responsible for that injury) for excess economic loss. Under the plan examined here, we assume that ANF electees purchase the mandated PPI policy limit. Thus, an ANF insured driver who injures someone else covered by ANF is liable for the victim's economic losses in excess of the PPI policy limit. An ANF insured driver who injures someone covered by the modified current system is liable for the victim's economic losses in excess of his or her TM policy limit. We assume that the distribution of TM policy limits purchased by consumers who elect the modified current system under choice is the same as the distribution of BI policy limits purchased by consumers under the current system. Because BI limits are at least as large as the mandated PPI limit, the expected excess economic losses incurred by victims who are covered by TM are less, on average, than the expected excess economic losses incurred by victims covered by PPI.

choice plan, drivers who choose the modified current system will have the same average noneconomic loss and negligence as do drivers who elect ANF, and these savings will approximately equal the additional costs.

Current no-fault plans already limit accident victims' access to compensation for noneconomic loss. Hence, the savings on compensation costs obtained by totally eliminating compensation payments for noneconomic loss on behalf of drivers who elect ANF are smaller than in tort states. But current no-fault plans already include PIP compensation, so no new compensation costs are incurred on behalf of drivers who elect ANF under choice in the no-fault states. Hence, compensation costs incurred on behalf of ANF electees in the no-fault states would also generally substantially decline relative to the costs incurred on their behalf under their state's current system. On average, the cost of compensating for personal injuries incurred or caused by insured drivers in the no-fault states who elect ANF would drop more than 45 percent in most states—relative to the costs incurred on their behalf under the current no-fault system. If insurers' other costs declined in proportion, the total premiums charged drivers who would be insured under the current system and would opt for ANF under choice would be reduced by more than 20 percent in most no-fault states.

The savings that would be realized by insured drivers who switch to ANF under choice are not very sensitive to the fraction of insured drivers who exercise that option. The estimated savings to drivers when 50 percent of insured drivers switch to ANF are very similar to the savings estimates when all insured drivers switch to ANF.

As in the tort states, drivers who elect the modified current system and are involved in an accident with a driver who chose ANF are entirely free from liability to the other driver for noneconomic loss; their insurers would pay out less, on average, under choice than under the current system. But drivers who chose the modified current system and are injured in an accident with a driver who chose ANF must turn to their own TM coverage for recovery of their own noneconomic losses. Their insurers save the costs of compensating the other driver for noneconomic loss but incur the additional costs of compensating the insured for his own noneconomic loss. If there is no adverse selection in the choices made under the choice plan, drivers who choose the modified current system will have the same average noneconomic loss and negligence as do drivers who elect ANF, and these savings will approximately equal the additional costs.

THE EFFECTS OF THE CHOICE PLAN ON COMPENSATION

Figure 3.1 draws on the results for the nominal case in California to illustrate the effects of the choice plan on compensation outcomes. The dark bars illustrate how $1,000 in compensation costs would be distributed in California under the current system. The dollar figure attached to each bar shows the amounts that would be spent on that cost category. The light bars illustrate how these compensation costs would be affected by the choice plan, assuming the nominal insurance parameters. The dollar figure attached to each of the light bars shows the amount that would be spent in each cost category under the choice system.

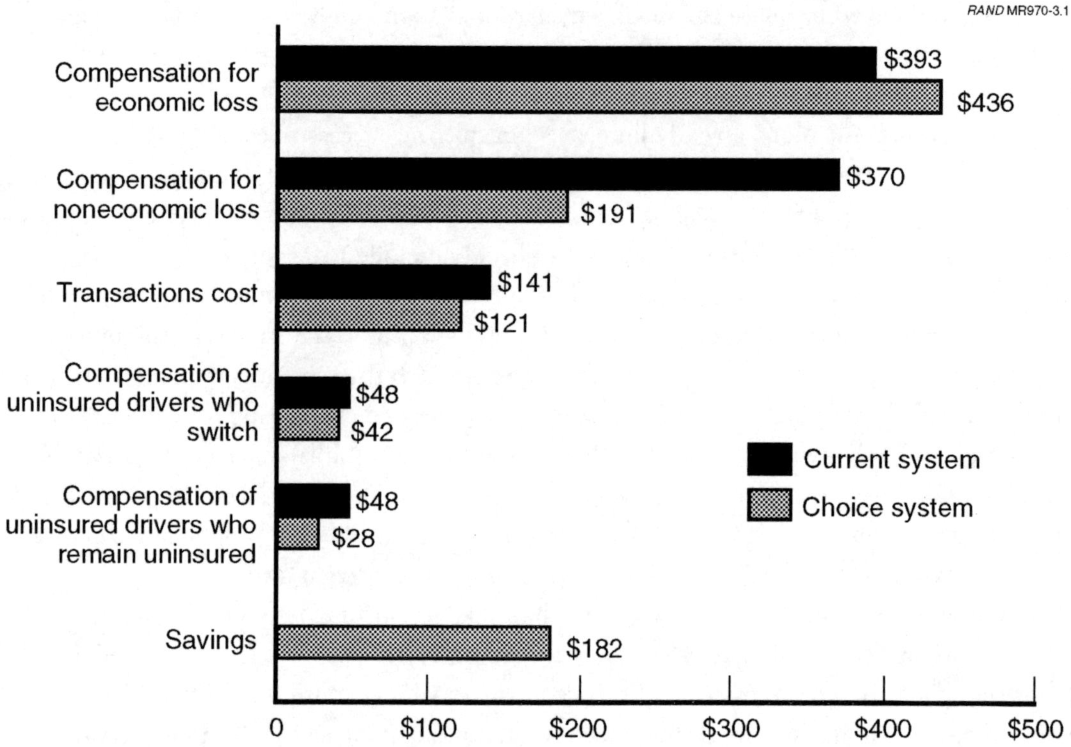

SOURCE: 1992 data for those compensated for automobile accidents.

Figure 3.1—Effects of Choice Plan on Compensation Outcomes in California

For purposes of this comparison, we count all dollars paid to accident victims as compensation for economic loss until they have been fully compensated; we include only amounts paid to victims in excess of their economic losses as compensation for noneconomic loss. The compensation figures are gross in that they show the amount paid to accident victims in compensation without regard to any legal fees or costs they must pay out of this amount. We distinguish between drivers who would be insured under the current system and those who would go uninsured under the current system. We divide the latter into two subgroups: those who stay uninsured under choice and those who elect to purchase ANF when it is available to them. (Because this illustration assumes that half of the uninsured drivers under the current system would switch to ANF under choice, these subgroups are equal in size.)

Out of each $1,000 spent in the current system, about $393 would be paid in compensation for economic loss to victims who have purchased insurance. Under choice, the amount of compensation paid to these victims for economic loss would be 11 percent greater, about $436. There are some differences from one victim to another in how the compensation paid to them for economic loss under the choice plan would compare with the compensation they would each have received under the current system.

About $370 out of each $1,000 spent in the current system would be paid to insured victims in compensation for noneconomic loss. Under choice, the amount of compensation paid to these victims for noneconomic loss would be cut to the extent that drivers switch to ANF. Drivers who elect the modified current system under choice would receive essentially the same compensation for noneconomic loss as under the current system, assuming no change in policy limits. Those who switch to ANF would receive no compensation for noneconomic loss. In the example, we assume that half the insured drivers under the current system elect the modified current system and half switch to ANF. Consequently, the amount paid to insured victims in compensation for noneconomic loss is reduced about half, to about $191 out of each $1,000 in compensation costs, under choice.

Insurers' transaction costs—defense fees and allocated loss adjustment expenses—account for about $141 out of each $1,000 under the current system. These costs would be cut about 15 percent, to about $121 out of each $1,000, under the choice plan for these assumed parameters. Note that the O'Connell et al. (1993) plan provides legal fees to ANF drivers who seek compensation for economic losses in excess of their PIP policy limits. Because this provision allows victims representation at no cost to themselves, we assume that victims will generally secure representation, even on small claims, increasing insurers' transaction costs for these claims.

The costs of compensating uninsured motorists under the current system account for $96 out of each $1,000 spent in the example. The choice plan would cut these costs about 27 percent. Uninsured drivers under the current system who switch to ANF under choice waive compensation for noneconomic loss in return for being assured compensation of economic loss. Uninsured switchers who would have gone uncompensated under the current system (e.g., an uninsured driver injured in a single-car accident) do better; they receive compensation for their economic loss. Uninsured switchers who would have obtained compensation from another driver's BI coverage for both their economic and noneconomic loss get less. The net result is a 12 percent reduction in the compensation paid to these victims, on average. The compensation paid to drivers who remain uninsured under choice is cut to 58 percent, on average, of what it would have been under the current system. Uninsured drivers under choice who are injured in an accident with someone who opted for the modified current system under choice receive the same compensation they would have received under the current system. But uninsured drivers under choice who are injured in an accident with someone who opted for ANF under choice are compensated only for their excess economic loss.

The effects of the plan on compensation outcomes generally follow the pattern described above for California.

SENSITIVITY ANALYSES

Sensitivity to Assumed Parameters

The estimates presented above are based on the assumed values of three critical parameters in each state:

1. The fraction of accidents that were the injured person's own fault (percent own-fault),
2. The fraction of accidents in which the injured person collects from both an at-fault other driver and from his own MP policy (percent claim-both), and
3. The fraction of drivers uninsured under the current system (percent uninsured).

To examine the sensitivity of our estimates to these parameters, we replicated the analysis for nine sets of assumptions made by combining the following:

- The percentage of own-fault accidents is 15, 30, or 60 percent,
- The percentage of claim-both victims is 25, 50, or 100 percent, and
- The percentage of uninsured motorists before choice is 10, 15, or 20 percent.

Table 3.4 presents the results of these calculations for the scenario in which 50 percent of insured drivers opt for ANF under choice. It shows the estimated reduction in total auto insurance premiums in tort states, no-fault states, and all states for each of the 27 alternative sets of assumptions.

As Table 3.4 shows, differences among these assumptions make very little difference in the overall results. Corresponding calculations for the scenario in which all insured drivers elect ANF under choice exhibit the same pattern. The estimates of the savings an individual driver who elects ANF will realize are insensitive to the underlying assumptions.

Sensitivity to Data Outliers

In each state, we find a few large settlements along with a large number of smaller ones. To see if this distribution posed a threat to our conclusions, we re-estimated the effects of the plan on insured switchers' compensation costs under each of the above 27 sets of assumptions, assuming, in every state and for each compensation element, that

- The compensation provided in each of the largest 10 percent of all cases is double the observed value,
- The compensation provided all cases, including that in the largest 10 percent of all cases, is the observed value, and
- The compensation provided in each of the largest 10 percent of all cases is half the observed value.

Table 3.5 compares relative savings under choice using each of the three sets of estimates, assuming that half of all insured drivers switch to ANF.[3] For example, we estimated that insured drivers in the tort states who switch to ANF under choice would see a 20 percent savings on their total premiums. When the compensation provided in the top 10 percent of all cases is doubled, this estimate falls to 18 percent. When it is cut in half, relative savings rise to 22 percent.

We combined each alternative value of each of the of the key parameters discussed above with alternative assumptions regarding the compensation provided in very large cases. In all, we considered all possible combinations of the three alternative assumptions regarding the percentage uninsured, the percentage own-fault, the percentage claim-both, and the distribution of very large cases to develop 81 estimates of the effects of the choice

---

[3]After some experimentation, we concluded that results are insensitive to changes in the lower distribution of costs (e.g., if we drop the bottom 10 percent of all cases, results change hardly at all).

plan on insured switchers' total auto insurance premiums in each state. Figure 3.2 shows the smallest, nominal, and largest of these estimates for each state, assuming that 50 percent of insured drivers elect ANF under choice. The left end of the bar shown for each state is the lowest estimate we obtained for the 81 cases for that state. The right end of the bar shown for each state is the highest estimate we obtained for the 81 cases for that state. The line inside the bar for a state shows the nominal estimate for that state. Figure 3.3 presents the corresponding figure for the scenario in which *all* insured drivers elect ANF under choice.

Table 3.4

Relative Savings for All Coverages for Insured Switchers Under Different Assumptions (in percent)

Own Fault Accidents	Collecting Medpay and BI	Uninsured Before Choice	Relative Savings: Tort States	No-Fault States	All States
		10	20.4	22.9	21.2
	25	15	21.2	23.6	22.0
		20	22.0	24.2	22.7
		10	18.3	21.5	19.3
15	50	15	19.2	22.1	20.1
		20	20.0	22.8	20.9
		10	11.2	17.0	13.1
	100	15	12.2	17.7	13.9
		20	13.1	18.3	14.7
		10	21.3	22.9	21.8
	25	15	22.0	23.6	22.5
		20	22.7	24.2	23.2
		10	19.3	21.5	20.0
30	50	15	20.0	22.1	20.7
		20	20.7	22.8	21.4
		10	12.3	17.0	13.8
	100	15	13.1	17.7	14.6
		20	13.9	18.3	15.3
		10	23.0	22.9	23.0
	25	15	23.5	23.6	23.5
		20	24.0	24.2	24.1
		10	21.0	21.5	21.2
60	50	15	21.6	22.1	21.8
		20	22.1	22.8	22.3
		10	14.2	17.0	15.1
	100	15	14.8	17.7	15.7
		20	15.5	18.3	16.3

SOURCE: 1992 data for those compensated for automobile accidents.

Table 3.5

Relative Savings for Insured Switchers Under Different Cost Estimates (in percent)

Premium	Cost Estimate	Tort States	No-Fault States	All States
	Half high compensation	50.0	51.3	50.5
Injury	Actual compensation	44.9	45.7	45.3
	Double high compensation	41.5	38.4	40.2
	Half high compensation	21.9	24.6	22.8
Total	Actual compensation	20.0	22.1	20.7
	Double high compensation	18.2	19.6	18.6

SOURCE: 1992 data for those compensated for automobile accidents.

For most states, the range of estimates is relatively small. Nothing in these estimates poses a serious threat to our main finding that the personal injury coverage costs of insuring drivers who elect ANF under choice will fall about 45 percent, which translates into savings of about 21 percent on their total premiums.

We used the same approach to develop 81 estimates of the effects of the choice plan on total auto insurance premiums to insured stayers—drivers who elect their state's modified current system—in each state. Figure 3.4 shows the smallest, nominal, and largest of these estimates for each state, assuming that 50 percent of insured drivers elect ANF under choice.

Here, too, the range of estimates is relatively small in most states. Nothing in these estimates poses a serious threat to our main finding that insured drivers who elect their state's modified current system under choice will not be noticeably affected by the availability of ANF.

Sensitivity to Other Assumptions

We assumed that insurance purchase decisions are statistically independent of subsequent accidents and the resulting injuries/losses. That is, we assume that bad drivers elect either the modified current system or ANF with the same probabilities as do good drivers. This is consistent with the available evidence in the three states that have adopted choice plans. There is no evidence that either particularly bad, or particularly good, drivers in any of these states self select into one or the other plan.

For that matter, the available evidence suggests that drivers may not have a clear understanding of their own relative driving performance. A national survey of people who suffered accidental injuries found that auto accident victims attributed their injuries to someone else more than 90 percent of the time and even drivers injured when their vehicle hit another vehicle named themselves as the cause of the accident only 16 percent of the time.[4] If drivers did not perceive themselves as having caused an accident in which they were injured, how likely is it that these same drivers would have labeled themselves before the fact as a driver likely to be involved in an accident? Self selection cannot affect the distribution of drivers between plans unless drivers accurately perceive their own driving ability.

[4]Hensler et al. (1991), p. 143.

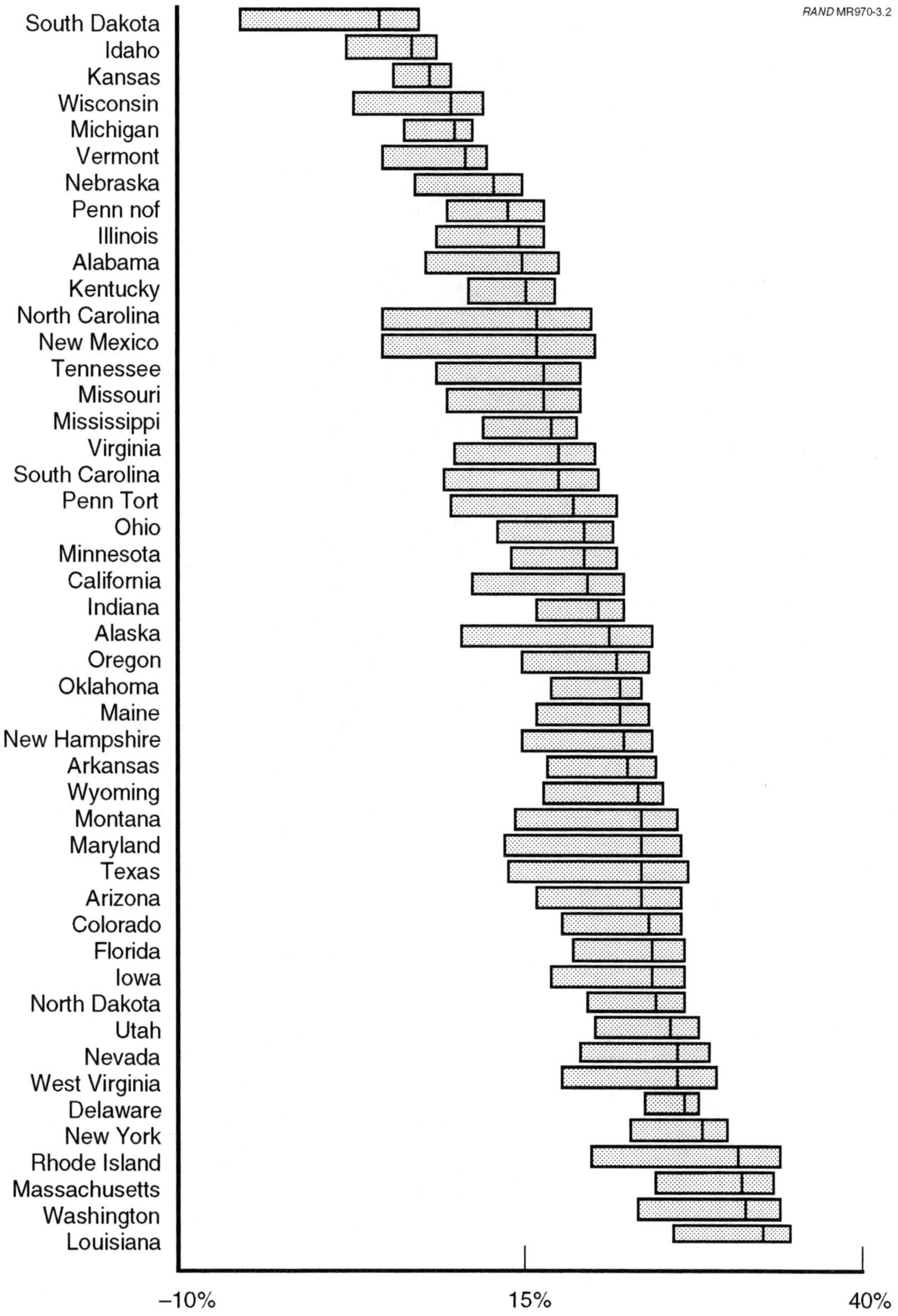

SOURCE: 1992 data for those compensated for automobile accidents.

Figure 3.2—Relative Savings for Drivers Who Switch If Half of Insured Drivers Switch to ANF: Smallest, Nominal, and Largest Percent Savings

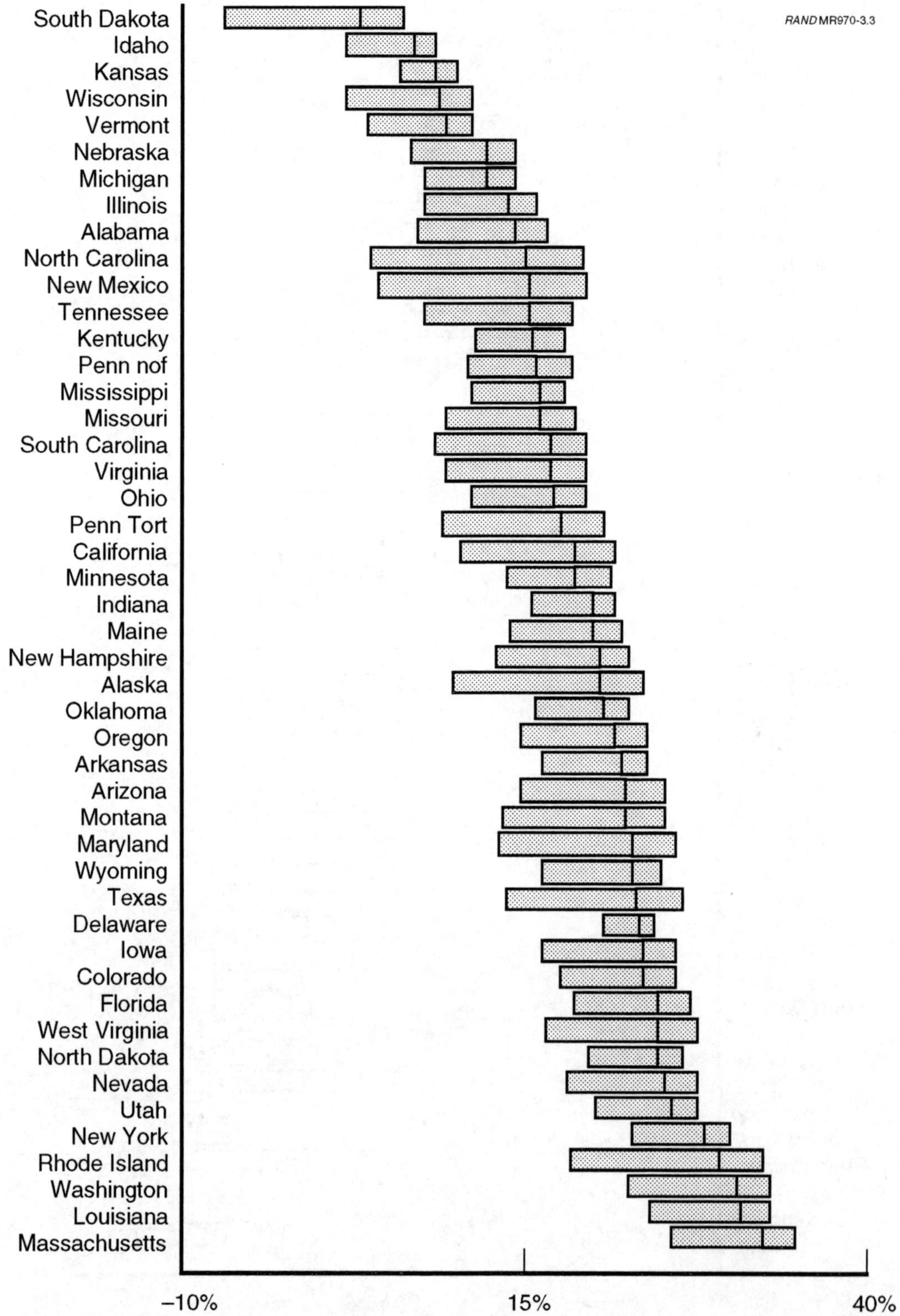

SOURCE: 1992 data for those compensated for automobile accidents.

Figure 3.3—Relative Savings for Drivers If All Insured Drivers Switch to ANF: Smallest, Nominal, and Largest Percent Savings

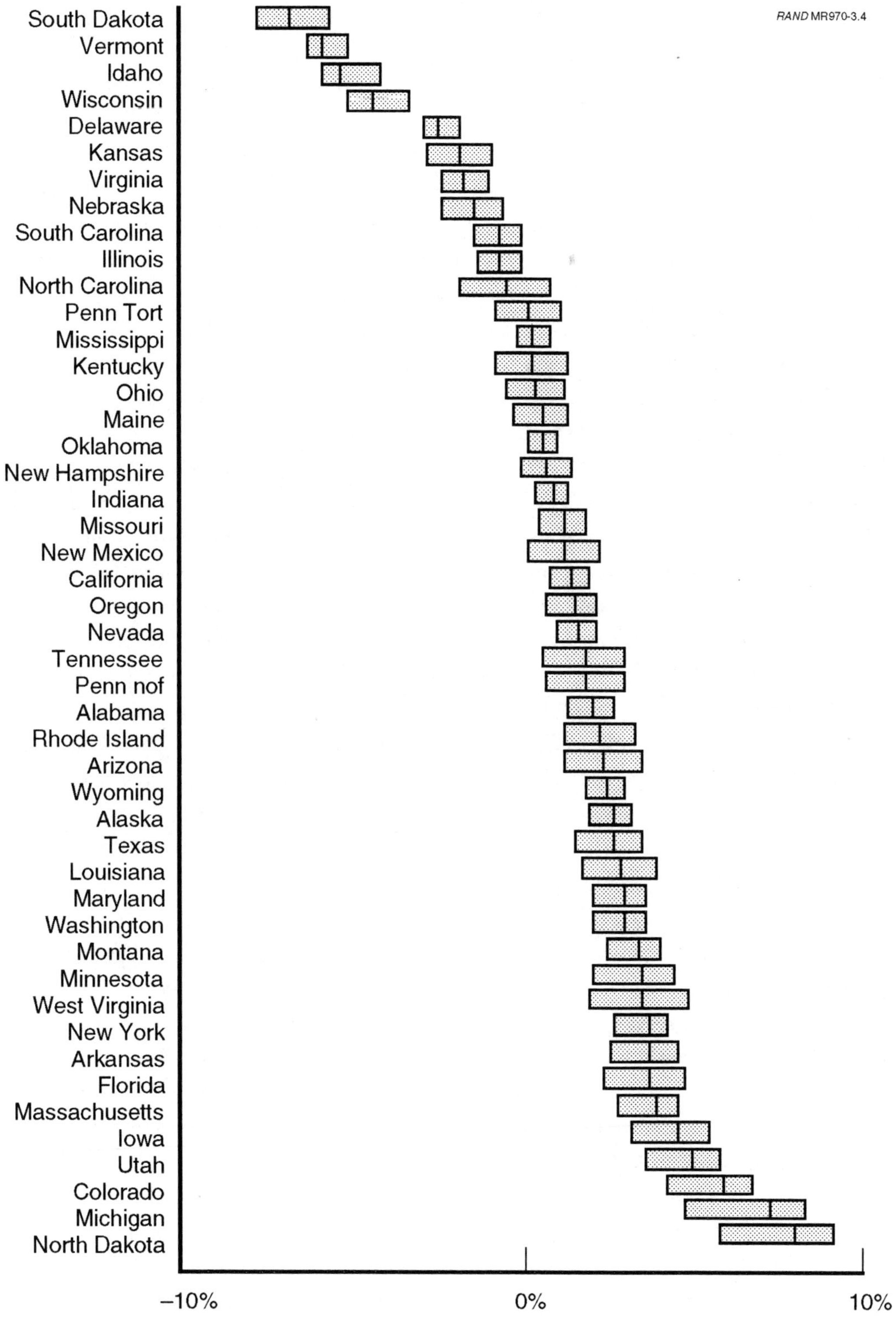

SOURCE: 1992 data for those compensated for automobile accidents.

Figure 3.4—Relative Savings for Drivers Who Retain a Modified Version of Their Current Insurance If Half of Insured Drivers Switch to ANF: Smallest, Nominal, and Largest Percent Savings

Finally, even if bad drivers, or good drivers, accurately perceived their own driving abilities, it is not clear which option they would prefer. Drivers covered by ANF who cause accidents impose costs on their insurers for their own economic losses, so insurers have the same incentives to experience-rate drivers who elect ANF under choice as they do to experience-rate drivers who elect the modified current system. Similarly, "accident-prone" drivers have to consider the tradeoff between the risk that the compensation available to them under the modified current system will be reduced to the degree that they are responsible for an accident in which they are injured and the loss of access to compensation for noneconomic loss if they elect ANF under choice.

Adverse selection is an empirical issue that warrants further study. However, the evidence now available offers no reason to suspect that adverse selection would be sufficient to dramatically affect the results.

The modification to the determination of which insurer is responsible for payment of the claim can affect the compensation that any particular accident victim receives, depending on the BI policy limits drivers would have purchased under the current system and the TM limits they would purchase if they elected the modified current system under choice. Suppose, for example, that driver A caused an accident in which driver B was injured. Under the current tort system (or no-fault system, if B's injury surmounts the threshold), B would be entitled to compensation for both economic and noneconomic losses from driver A's insurer under A's BI coverage. If B's losses were less than A's BI policy limit, B would fully recover. If B's losses exceeded the BI policy limit, B would receive compensation equal to the policy limit from A's insurer and go uncompensated to the extent that his or her losses exceeded the limit. In principle, B would be entitled to pursue an action against A's personal assets for the difference. But, in practice, the amount of compensation paid by individuals to people they harmed in auto accidents appears to be negligible.[5]

Now suppose this accident had occurred in a choice environment in which A had elected ANF and B had elected the modified current system. B would be entitled to compensation for both economic and noneconomic losses, but, under the modified system B's insurer would be responsible for payment under B's TM coverage. If B's losses were less than the TM policy limits he or she had purchased, B would fully recover. If B's losses exceeded the TM policy limit, B would receive compensation equal to the TM policy limit from his or her insurer. If B's compensation under the TM policy was less than B's economic loss, B could seek payment of the uncompensated economic loss from A's insurer under A's BI coverage, to the limits of that coverage.

Clearly, if B's economic and noneconomic losses add up to less than the state's financial responsibility (FR) requirement, the above distinctions are irrelevant. B is fully compensated in either case. And the cost of compensating B is the same in either case. If B's total loss exceeds the FR, he or she would be better (or worse) off, and costs would be correspondingly greater (or lower) under the modified system if the BI policy limits that A

---

[5]A national survey of auto accident victims found that over 98 percent of the compensation they received was paid by some form of insurance—auto, health, workers' compensation, or disability—or government sources. All other sources of compensation combined accounted for less than 2 percent of the compensation accident victims received. See Insurance Research Council (May 1994).

would have purchased had choice not been introduced are greater (lower) than the TM policy limits B would purchase under the choice plan.

4. CONCLUSIONS

Because we focus on the financial implications of the choice plan, our work does not address the degree to which accident victims derive satisfaction from being compensated under an insurance policy purchased by the driver who injured them.[1] Nor do we consider the satisfaction that consumers who value access to compensation for noneconomic loss derive from being able to determine for themselves the limits on what they can obtain if injured by another driver in an auto accident rather facing the uncertainty of the policy limit purchased by that driver.

Our results, however, do suggest that the choice plan can deliver on its promise to offer dramatically less expensive insurance to drivers willing to give up access to compensation for noneconomic loss with little actual effect on those who want to retain access to compensation for both economic and noneconomic loss. If insurers pass on cost savings, the adoption of a choice plan would

- Allow drivers who are willing to waive their tort rights to buy ANF personal injury coverage for roughly 45 percent of what they have to pay for personal injury coverage under their state's current system, which translates into savings on total premiums of about 21 percent on their total premiums, on average, and
- Allow drivers who preferred to remain within a somewhat modified version of their state's current system to do so, at essentially the same costs as under their state's current system.

---

[1]See Hensler et al. (1991), Section V, for a review of the literature on the factors that motivate claiming.

Appendix A
TECHNICAL DETAILS

If

f = fraction no other at fault driver,
b = fraction uninsured, and
g = fraction claiming both medpay and personal injury,

then Table A.1 is the distribution of accident victims.

Table A.1
Distribution of Accident Victims

Accident Victim	Other Driver at Least Partially at Fault: Uninsured	Other Driver at Least Partially at Fault: Insured	No Other Driver at Fault
Uninsured	$(1 - f)b^2$	$(1 - f)(1 - b)b$	fb
Insured	$(1 - f)(1 - b)b$	$(1 - f)(1 - b)^2$	$f(1 - b)$

Now suppose that for any particular coverage (e.g., medical payments), the probability that *if* an accident falls in cell row i, column j, of Table A.1, *then* a claim will be made under that coverage is g_{ij}. We call these g's the claiming probabilities for this form of coverage.

If the total number of accidents is A, then the total number of claims under this coverage is

$$C = A\Sigma p_{ij}g_{ij}$$

where p_{ij} is the probability displayed in row i, column j, of Table A.1.

Now suppose it is known that a total of C claims were made for a particular form of coverage. Then, of course,

$$A = C/\Sigma p_{ij}g_{ij}$$

and the number of claims under this coverage that we would see in row i, column j, of Table A.1 would be

$$C_{ij} = Ap_{ij}g_{ij} = Cp_{ij}g_{ij}/\Sigma p_{ij}g_{ij} \qquad (1)$$

UNINSURED MOTORIST CLAIMS

Only an insured accident victim involved with another driver who is at least partially at fault will make a UM claim. Therefore, all uninsured motorist claims fall into the second row, first column, of Table A.1.

BODILY INJURY CLAIMS

A BI claim can be made only if there is another driver who is at least partially at fault and is insured. Such a claim can be made regardless of the insurance status of the accident victim. Therefore, all personal injury claims fall into the two cells in the second column of Table A.1. Applying Eq. (1), the number of bodily injury claims in each cell of the matrix is given in Table A.2.

Table A.2

Distribution of BI Claims

Accident Victim	Other Driver at Least Partially at Fault: Uninsured	Other Driver at Least Partially at Fault: Insured	No Other Driver at Fault
Uninsured		bB	
Insured		(1 – b)B	

where B is the number of BI claims.

MEDICAL PAYMENTS/PERSONAL INJURY PROTECTION

In a tort (no-fault) state, a MP (PIP) claim may be made under two different circumstances:

- First, the accident victim is insured and there is no other driver at fault, and
- Second, the accident victim is insured, there is an insured other driver who is at least partially at fault (the victim's injury exceeds the threshold), and the accident victim chooses to claim under both his or her own MP (PIP) policy and the other driver's policy.

Therefore, all MP (PIP) claims fall into the cells in the second row, second and third columns, of Table A.1. Applying Eq. (1), if there are P MP (PIP) claims, the number of such claims in each cell of the matrix is given in Table A.3.

Table A.3

Distribution of MP (PIP) Claims

Accident Victim	Other Driver at Least Partially at Fault: Uninsured	Other Driver at Least Partially at Fault: Insured	No Other Driver at Fault
Uninsured			
Insured		(1 – b)(1 – f)gP/D	fP/D

where P = number of MP/PIP claims, and D = (1 – b)(1 – f)g + f.

DISTRIBUTION OF PERSONAL INJURY CLAIMS

Given a particular number of bodily injury, medical payment/personal injury protection, and uninsured motorist claims, these claims will fall into the six cells of Table A.1 according to the formulas given in Table A.4.

Table A.4

Distribution of Claims Under the Current System

Accident Victim	Other Driver at Least Partially at Fault: Uninsured	Other Driver at Least Partially at Fault: Insured	No Other Driver at Fault
Uninsured		bB	
Insured	U	(1 – b)B + (1 – b)(1 – f)gP/D	fP/D

Appendix B

WHY THE 1992 RESULTS DIFFER FROM THE 1987 RESULTS

In the tort states, automobile insurance compensates accident victims for both economic and noneconomic losses, up to the limits of the applicable insurance policy, to the degree the insured is at fault for the victims' injuries. In the no-fault states, accident victims' own PIP insurance compensates them for their economic losses, up to the policy limits. Victims whose injuries/losses exceed the threshold can also seek compensation for noneconomic losses from drivers who caused their injuries, up to the limits on the applicable insurance policy, to the degree those drivers are at fault. Notwithstanding their rights to compensation for noneconomic losses, the amount accident victims can actually recover for those losses, in either case, depends on the difference between their own economic losses and the injuror's policy limits.

Under the choice plan, if all insureds opt for ANF, an accident victim would be compensated only for economic loss, but many of those whose compensation would formerly have been capped by policy limits would be more fully compensated, at greater expense to the insurance system. Thus, the plan "saves" money, relative to the current system, with respect to any victim who would have been compensated for noneconomic loss because it would not provide him or her that compensation. It "loses" money relative to the current system with respect to any victim who would not have been fully compensated for economic loss because it provides him or her full compensation for economic loss, to the policy limit.

Claimed economic losses have increased since 1987. The accident victims in our 1992 database claimed economic losses that were much greater, on average, than the losses claimed by the accident victims in our 1987 database.[1] Figure B.1 illustrates the change in the distribution of claimed economic losses between 1987 and 1992. It shows the distributions of claimed economic losses in California in each of those years.

But drivers have generally not increased their policy limits to keep pace with the rate of growth in claimed losses. As a greater fraction of 1992 accident victims' economic loss claims neared insurance policy limits, compensation from auto insurance grew at a slower rate than did economic loss claims.[2]

---

[1]In California, for example, in 1987, accident victims claimed an average of $5,433 (in 1987 dollars) in economic losses. In 1992, California accident victims claimed an average of $10,286 (in 1992 dollars) in economic losses.

[2]The ratio of auto insurance compensation to economic loss in California fell from 1.04, in 1987, to 0.88, in 1992.

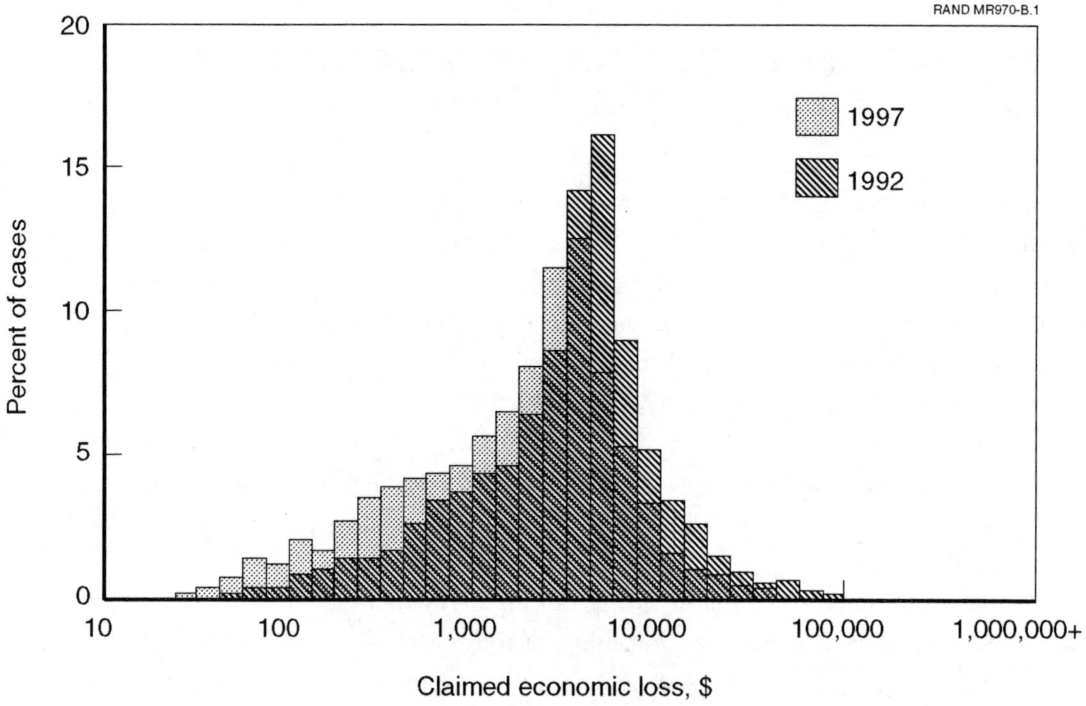

Figure B.1—Upward Creep of Claimed Economic Loss Distributions: California, 1987 and 1992

Consequently, our updated estimate of the costs of compensating auto accident victims under the choice plan are greater and, hence, our updated estimates of the plan's savings, lower, than our earlier estimates based on 1987 data.

Table B.1 illustrates this shift by considering how hypothetical California auto accident victims injured by an insured driver who purchased a $15,000 BI policy (the financial responsibility level in California) would be compensated under the current system and under the choice plan, assuming that they opted for ANF. For simplicity, assume that the victim had no responsibility for the accident.

Table B.1

Hypothetical Examples of Compensation Under the Current and Proposed Plans (in $ thousands)

		Compensation	Compensation Under Choice Plan		
	Economic	Under Current	PPI	BI	
Victim	Loss	System	Compensation	Compensation	Savings
A	2	6	2	0	4
B	10	15	10	0	5
C	25	15	15	10	–10
D	100	15	15	15	–15

Accident victim A incurred $2,000 in economic loss. Under the current system, he would be compensated for his economic losses and would receive something, say $4,000, for his noneconomic losses. Under the choice plan he would receive only $2,000 for his economic losses, a savings of $4,000 compared to the current system. Accident victim B incurred $10,000 in economic loss. Under the current system, he would be compensated for his economic losses and, because he was injured by a driver whose policy limit was $15,000, would receive $5,000, at most, for his noneconomic losses. Under the choice plan he would receive only $10,000 for his economic losses, a savings of $5,000 over that of the current system. Accident victim C incurred $25,000 in economic loss. Because he was injured by a driver whose policy limit was $15,000, he would receive only $15,000 for his economic losses under the current system. Under the choice plan, his PPI coverage would pay $15,000 of his economic loss; he could recover $10,000 from the other driver's supplemental BI coverage for his excess economic losses. In all, auto insurers would pay out $10,000 more under ANF than under the current system. Finally, accident victim D incurred $100,000 in economic loss. Under the current system, because he was injured by a driver whose policy limit was $15,000, he would receive only $15,000 from auto insurance. Under the choice plan, he would receive $15,000 from his PIP coverage and $15,000 from the other driver's supplemental BI coverage for excess economic losses. In all, auto insurers would pay out $15,000 more under ANF than under the current system.[3]

Compared to the current system, the choice plan "saves" on victims A and B and "loses" on victims C and D. Between 1987 and 1992, the distribution of accident victims shifted so that relatively fewer are like A or B and relatively more are like C or D.

[3]If victims C or D had UIM coverage, they would receive additional compensation under the current system under that coverage. However, because many consumers do not purchase UIM coverage, that does not affect the basic point of the example.

BIBLIOGRAPHY

Abrahamse, Allan, and Stephen J. Carroll, *The Effects of a Choice Automobile Insurance Plan Under Consideration by the Joint Economic Committee of the United States Congress,* Santa Monica, CA: RAND, DRU-1609-ICJ, April 1997.

Abrahamse, Allan, and Stephen J. Carroll, *The Effects of a Choice Auto Insurance Plan on Insurance Costs,* Santa Monica, CA: RAND, MR-540-ICJ, 1995.

All-Industry Research Advisory Council, *Uninsured Motorists,* Oak Brook, IL: 1989.

Carroll, Stephen J., et al., *The Costs of Excess Medical Claims for Automobile Personal Injuries,* Santa Monica, CA: RAND, DB-139-ICJ, 1995.

Carroll, Stephen J., and James Kakalik, "No-Fault Approaches to Compensating Auto Accident Victims," *Journal of Risk and Insurance,* Vol. 60, No. 2, 1993, pp. 265–287.

Carroll, Stephen J., et al., *No-Fault Approaches to Compensating People Injured in Automobile Accidents,* Santa Monica, CA: RAND, R-4019-ICJ, 1991.

Hensler, Deborah R., et al., *Compensation for Accidental Injuries in the United States,* Santa Monica, CA: RAND, R-3999-HHS/ICJ, 1991.

Insurance Research Council, *Fraud and Buildup in Auto Insurance Claims,* Wheaton, IL: September 1996.

Insurance Research Council, *Paying for Auto Injuries,* Oak Brook, IL: Insurance Research Council, May 1994.

Insurance Research Council, *Auto Injuries: Claiming Behavior and Its Impact on Insurance Costs,* Oak Brook, IL: Insurance Research Council, September 1994.

National Association of Independent Insurers, *Private Passenger Automobile Experience,* Des Plaines, IL: 1995.

National Association of Insurance Commissioners, *State Average Expenditures and Premiums for Personal Automobile Insurance in 1995,* Kansas City, MO: 1997.

O'Connell, Jeffrey, Stephen J. Carroll, Michael Horowitz, Allan Abrahamse, and Paul Jamieson, "The Comparative Costs of Allowing Consumer Choice for Auto Insurance in all Fifty States," *Maryland Law Review,* Vol. 55, No. 1, 1996, pp. 160–222.

O'Connell, Jeffrey, Stephen J. Carroll, Michael Horowitz, and Allan Abrahamse, "Consumer Choice in the Auto Insurance Market," *Maryland Law Review*, Vol. 52, No. 4, 1993, pp. 1016–1062.

O'Connell, Jeffrey, and Robert H. Joost, "Giving Motorists a Choice Between Fault and No-fault Insurance," *Virginia Law Review,* Vol. 72, No. 1, 1986, pp. 61–89.

ICJ PUBLICATIONS

OUTCOMES

General

Carroll, S. J., with N. M. Pace, *Assessing the Effects of Tort Reforms*, R-3554-ICJ, 1987. $7.50.

Galanter, M., B. Garth, D. Hensler, and F. K. Zemans, *How to Improve Civil Justice Policy*, RP-282. (Reprinted from *Judicature*, Vol. 77, No. 4, January/February 1994.) Free.

Hensler, D. R., *Summary of Research Results on the Tort Liability System*, P-7210-ICJ, 1986. (Testimony before the Committee on Commerce, Science, and Transportation, United States Senate, February 1986.) $4.00.

———, *Trends in California Tort Liability Litigation*, P-7287-ICJ, 1987. (Testimony before the Select Committee on Insurance, California State Assembly, October 1987.) $4.00.

———, *Researching Civil Justice: Problems and Pitfalls*, P-7604-ICJ, 1988. (Reprinted from *Law and Contemporary Problems*, Vol. 51, No. 3, Summer 1988.) $4.00.

———, *Reading the Tort Litigation Tea Leaves: What's Going on in the Civil Liability System?* RP-226. (Reprinted from *The Justice System Journal*, Vol. 16, No. 2, 1993.) Free.

———, *Why We Don't Know More About the Civil Justice System—and What We Could Do About It*, RP-363, 1995. (Reprinted from *USC Law*, Fall 1994.) Free.

Hensler, D. R., and E. Moller, *Trends in Punitive Damages: Preliminary Data from Cook County, Illinois, and San Francisco, California,* DRU-1014-ICJ, 1995. Free.

Hensler, D. R., M. E. Vaiana, J. S. Kakalik, and M. A. Peterson, *Trends in Tort Litigation: The Story Behind the Statistics*, R-3583-ICJ, 1987. $4.00.

Hill, P. T., and D. L. Madey, *Educational Policymaking Through the Civil Justice System*, R-2904-ICJ, 1982. $4.00.

Lipson, A. J., *California Enacts Prejudgment Interest: A Case Study of Legislative Action*, N-2096-ICJ, 1984. $4.00.

Moller, E., *Trends in Punitive Damages: Preliminary Data from California*, DRU-1059-ICJ, 1995. Free.

Shubert, G. H., *Some Observations on the Need for Tort Reform,* P-7189-ICJ, 1986. (Testimony before the National Conference of State Legislatures, January 1986.) $4.00.

———, *Changes in the Tort System: Helping Inform the Policy Debate,* P-7241-ICJ, 1986. $4.00.

Jury Verdicts

Bailis, D. S., and R. J. MacCoun, *Estimating Liability Risks with the Media as Your Guide,* RP-606, 1996. (Reprinted from *Law and Human Behavior,* Vol. 20, No. 4, 1996, pp. 419–429.) Free.

Carroll, S. J., *Jury Awards and Prejudgment Interest in Tort Cases*, N-1994-ICJ, 1983. $4.00.

———, *Punitive Damages in Financial Injury Jury Verdicts,* CT-143, June 1997. (Written statement delivered on June 24, 1997, to the Judiciary Committee of the United States Senate.) $5.00.

Chin, A., and M. A. Peterson, *Deep Pockets, Empty Pockets: Who Wins in Cook County Jury Trials*, R-3249-ICJ, 1985. $10.00.

Dertouzos, J. N., E. Holland, and P. A. Ebener, *The Legal and Economic Consequences of Wrongful Termination*, R-3602-ICJ, 1988. $7.50.

Hensler, D. R., *Summary of Research Results on the Tort Liability System,* P-7210-ICJ, 1986. (Testimony before the Committee on Commerce, Science, and Transportation, United States Senate, February 1986.) $4.00.

Hensler, D. R., and E. Moller, *Trends in Punitive Damages: Preliminary Data from Cook County, Illinois, and San Francisco, California,* DRU-1014-ICJ, 1995. Free.

MacCoun, R. J., *Getting Inside the Black Box: Toward a Better Understanding of Civil Jury Behavior*, N-2671-ICJ, 1987. $4.00.

———, *Experimental Research on Jury Decisionmaking*, R-3832-ICJ, 1989. (Reprinted from *Science*, Vol. 244, June 1989.) $4.00.

———, *Inside the Black Box: What Empirical Research Tells Us About Decisionmaking by Civil Juries*, RP-238, 1993. (Reprinted from Robert E. Litan, ed., *Verdict: Assessing the Civil Jury System*, The Brookings Institution, 1993.) Free.

———, *Is There a "Deep-Pocket" Bias in the Tort System?* IP-130, October 1993. Free.

———, *Blaming Others to a Fault?* RP-286. (Reprinted from *Chance*, Vol. 6, No. 4, Fall 1993.) Free.

———, *Improving Jury Comprehension in Criminal and Civil Trials,* CT-136, July 1995. $5.00.

Moller, E., *Trends in Punitive Damages: Preliminary Data from California,* DRU-1059-ICJ, 1995. Free.

———, *Trends in Civil Jury Verdicts Since 1985,* MR-694-ICJ, 1996. $15.00.

Moller, E., N. M. Pace, and S. J. Carroll, *Punitive Damages in Financial Injury Jury Verdicts,* MR-888-ICJ, 1997. $9.00

———, *Punitive Damages in Financial Injury Jury Verdicts: Executive Summary,* MR-889-ICJ, 1997. $15.00.

Peterson, M. A., *Compensation of Injuries: Civil Jury Verdicts in Cook County*, R-3011-ICJ, 1984. $7.50.

———, *Punitive Damages: Preliminary Empirical Findings*, N-2342-ICJ, 1985. $4.00.

———, *Summary of Research Results: Trends and Patterns in Civil Jury Verdicts,* P-7222-ICJ, 1986. (Testimony before the Subcommittee on Oversight, Committee on Ways and Means, United States House of Representatives, March 1986.) $4.00.

———, *Civil Juries in the 1980s: Trends in Jury Trials and Verdicts in California and Cook County, Illinois*, R-3466-ICJ, 1987. $7.50.

Peterson, M. A., and G. L. Priest, *The Civil Jury: Trends in Trials and Verdicts, Cook County, Illinois, 1960–1979*, R-2881-ICJ, 1982. $7.50.

Peterson, M. A., S. Sarma, and M. G. Shanley, *Punitive Damages: Empirical Findings*, R-3311-ICJ, 1987. $7.50.

Selvin, M., and L. Picus, *The Debate over Jury Performance: Observations from a Recent Asbestos Case*, R-3479-ICJ, 1987. $10.00.

Shanley, M. G., and M. A. Peterson, *Comparative Justice: Civil Jury Verdicts in San Francisco and Cook Counties, 1959–1980*, R-3006-ICJ, 1983. $7.50.

———, *Posttrial Adjustments to Jury Awards*, R-3511-ICJ, 1987. $7.50.

Costs of Dispute Resolution

Dunworth, T., and J. S. Kakalik, Preliminary Observations on Implementation of the Pilot Program of the Civil Justice Reform Act of 1990, RP-361, 1995. (Reprinted from Stanford Law Review, Vol. 46, No. 6, July 1994.) Free.

Hensler, D. R., Does ADR Really Save Money? The Jury's Still Out, RP-327, 1994. (Reprinted from The National Law Journal, April 11, 1994.) Free.

Hensler, D. R., M. E. Vaiana, J. S. Kakalik, and M. A. Peterson, Trends in Tort Litigation: The Story Behind the Statistics, R-3583-ICJ, 1987. $4.00.

Kakalik, J. S., and A. E. Robyn, Costs of the Civil Justice System: Court Expenditures for Processing Tort Cases, R-2888-ICJ, 1982. $7.50.

Kakalik, J. S., and R. L. Ross, Costs of the Civil Justice System: Court Expenditures for Various Types of Civil Cases, R-2985-ICJ, 1983. $10.00.

Kakalik, J. S., P. A. Ebener, W. L. F. Felstiner, and M. G. Shanley, Costs of Asbestos Litigation, R-3042-ICJ, 1983. $4.00.

Kakalik, J. S., P. A. Ebener, W. L. F. Felstiner, G. W. Haggstrom, and M. G. Shanley, Variation in Asbestos Litigation Compensation and Expenses, R-3132-ICJ, 1984. $7.50.

Kakalik, J. S., and N. M. Pace, Costs and Compensation Paid in Tort Litigation, R-3391-ICJ, 1986. $15.00.

———, Costs and Compensation Paid in Tort Litigation, P-7243-ICJ, 1986. (Testimony before the Subcommittee on Trade, Productivity, and Economic Growth, Joint Economic Committee of the Congress, July 1986.) $4.00.

Kakalik, J. S., E. M. King, M. Traynor, P. A. Ebener, and L. Picus, Costs and Compensation Paid in Aviation Accident Litigation, R-3421-ICJ, 1988. $10.00.

Kakalik, J. S., M. Selvin, and N. M. Pace, Averting Gridlock: Strategies for Reducing Civil Delay in the Los Angeles Superior Court, R-3762-ICJ, 1990. $10.00.

Kakalik, J. S., T. Dunworth, L. A. Hill, D. McCaffrey, M. Oshiro, N. M. Pace, and M. E. Vaiana, Just, Speedy, and Inexpensive? An Evaluation of Judicial Case Management Under the Civil Justice Reform Act, MR-800-ICJ, 1996. $8.00.

Kakalik, J. S., T. Dunworth, L. A. Hill, D. McCaffrey, M. Oshiro, N. M. Pace, and M. E. Vaiana, Implementation of the Civil Justice Reform Act in Pilot and Comparison Districts, MR-801-ICJ, 1996. $20.00.

Kakalik, J. S., T. Dunworth, L. A. Hill, D. McCaffrey, M. Oshiro, N. M. Pace, and M. E. Vaiana, An Evaluation of Judicial Case Management Under the Civil Justice Reform Act, MR-802-ICJ, 1996. $20.00.

Kakalik, J. S., T. Dunworth, L.A. Hill, D. McCaffrey, M. Oshiro, N. M. Pace, and M.E. Vaiana, *An Evaluation of Mediation and Early Neutral Evaluation Under the Civil Justice Reform Act,* MR-803-ICJ, 1996. $20.00.

Lind, E. A., *Arbitrating High-Stakes Cases: An Evaluation of Court-Annexed Arbitration in a United States District Court,* R-3809-ICJ, 1990. $10.00.

MacCoun, R. J., E. A. Lind, D. R. Hensler, D. L. Bryant, and P. A. Ebener, *Alternative Adjudication: An Evaluation of the New Jersey Automobile Arbitration Program,* R-3676-ICJ, 1988. $10.00.

Peterson, M. A., *New Tools for Reducing Civil Litigation Expenses,* R-3013-ICJ, 1983. $4.00.

Priest, G. L., *Regulating the Content and Volume of Litigation: An Economic Analysis,* R-3084-ICJ, 1983. $4.00.

DISPUTE RESOLUTION

Court Delay

Adler, J. W., W. L. F. Felstiner, D. R. Hensler, and M. A. Peterson, *The Pace of Litigation: Conference Proceedings*, R-2922-ICJ, 1982. $10.00.

Dunworth, T., and J. S. Kakalik, *Preliminary Observations on Implementation of the Pilot Program of the Civil Justice Reform Act of 1990,* RP-361, 1995. (Reprinted from *Stanford Law Review,* Vol. 46, No. 6, July 1994.) Free.

Dunworth, T., and N. M. Pace, *Statistical Overview of Civil Litigation in the Federal Courts,* R-3885-ICJ, 1990. $7.50.

Ebener, P. A., J. Wilson-Adler, M. Selvin, and M. S. Yeasley, *Court Efforts to Reduce Pretrial Delay: A National Inventory,* R-2732-ICJ, 1981. $10.00.

Kakalik, J. S., *Just, Speedy, and Inexpensive? Judicial Case Management Under the Civil Justice Reform Act,* RP-635, 1997. (Reprinted from *Judicature,* Vol. 80, No. 4, January–February 1997, pp. 184–189.) Free.

Kakalik, J. S., D. R. Hensler, D. McCaffrey, M. Oshiro, N. M. Pace, and M. E. Vaiana, *Discovery Management: Further Analysis of the Civil Justice Reform Act Evaluation Data,* MR-941-ICJ, 1997. $15.00.

Kakalik, J. S., M. Selvin, and N. M. Pace, *Averting Gridlock: Strategies for Reducing Civil Delay in the Los Angeles Superior Court,* R-3762-ICJ, 1990. $10.00.

———, Strategies for Reducing Civil Delay in the Los Angeles Superior Court: Technical Appendixes, N-2988-ICJ, 1990. $10.00.

Kakalik, J. S., T. Dunworth, L. A. Hill, D. McCaffrey, M. Oshiro, N. M. Pace, and M. E. Vaiana, Just, Speedy, and Inexpensive? An Evaluation of Judicial Case Management Under the Civil Justice Reform Act, MR-800-ICJ, 1996. $8.00.

Kakalik, J. S., T. Dunworth, L. A. Hill, D. McCaffrey, M. Oshiro, N. M. Pace, and M. E. Vaiana, Implementation of the Civil Justice Reform Act in Pilot and Comparison Districts, MR-801-ICJ, 1996. $20.00.

Kakalik, J. S., T. Dunworth, L. A. Hill, D. McCaffrey, M. Oshiro, N. M. Pace, and M. E. Vaiana, An Evaluation of Judicial Case Management Under the Civil Justice Reform Act, MR-802-ICJ, 1996. $20.00.

Kakalik, J. S., T. Dunworth, L. A. Hill, D. McCaffrey, M. Oshiro, N. M. Pace, and M. E. Vaiana, An Evaluation of Mediation and Early Neutral Evaluation Under the Civil Justice Reform Act, MR-803-ICJ, 1996. $20.00.

Lind, E. A., Arbitrating High-Stakes Cases: An Evaluation of Court-Annexed Arbitration in a United States District Court, R-3809-ICJ, 1990. $10.00.

MacCoun, R. J., E. A. Lind, D. R. Hensler, D. L. Bryant, and P. A. Ebener, Alternative Adjudication: An Evaluation of the New Jersey Automobile Arbitration Program, R-3676-ICJ, 1988. $10.00.

Resnik, J., Managerial Judges, R-3002-ICJ, 1982. (Reprinted from the Harvard Law Review, Vol. 96, No. 374, December 1982.) $7.50.

Selvin, M., and P. A. Ebener, Managing the Unmanageable: A History of Civil Delay in the Los Angeles Superior Court, R-3165-ICJ, 1984. $15.00.

Alternative Dispute Resolution

Adler, J. W., D. R. Hensler, and C. E. Nelson, with the assistance of G. J. Rest, *Simple Justice: How Litigants Fare in the Pittsburgh Court Arbitration Program*, R-3071-ICJ, 1983. $15.00.

Bryant, D. L., *Judicial Arbitration in California: An Update*, N-2909-ICJ, 1989. $4.00.

Ebener, P. A., and D. R. Betancourt, *Court-Annexed Arbitration: The National Picture*, N-2257-ICJ, 1985. $25.00.

Hensler, D. R., *Court-Annexed Arbitration in the State Trial Court System*, P-6963-ICJ, 1984. (Testimony before the Judiciary Committee Subcommittee on Courts, United States Senate, February 1984.) $4.00.

———, Reforming the Civil Litigation Process: How Court Arbitration Can Help, P-7027-ICJ, 1984. (Reprinted from the New Jersey Bell Journal, August 1984.) $4.00.

———, What We Know and Don't Know About Court-Administered Arbitration, N-2444-ICJ, 1986. $4.00.

———, Court-Ordered Arbitration: An Alternative View, RP-103, 1992. (Reprinted from The University of Chicago Legal Forum, Vol. 1990, 1990.) Free.

———, Science in the Court: Is There a Role for Alternative Dispute Resolution? RP-109, 1992. (Reprinted from Law and Contemporary Problems, Vol. 54, No. 3, Summer 1991.) Free.

———, Does ADR Really Save Money? The Jury's Still Out, RP-327, 1994. (Reprinted from The National Law Journal, April 11, 1994.) Free.

———, A Glass Half Full, a Glass Half Empty: The Use of Alternative Dispute Resolution in Mass Personal Injury Litigation, RP-446, 1995. (Reprinted from Texas Law Review, Vol. 73, No. 7, June 1995.) Free.

Hensler, D. R., A. J. Lipson, and E. S. Rolph, Judicial Arbitration in California: The First Year, R-2733-ICJ, 1981. $10.00.

———, Judicial Arbitration in California: The First Year: Executive Summary, R-2733/1-ICJ, 1981. $4.00.

Hensler, D. R., and J. W. Adler, with the assistance of G. J. Rest, Court-Administered Arbitration: An Alternative for Consumer Dispute Resolution, N-1965-ICJ, 1983. $4.00.

Kakalik, J. S., T. Dunworth, L. A. Hill, D. McCaffrey, M. Oshiro, N. M. Pace, and M. E. Vaiana, An Evaluation of Mediation and Early Neutral Evaluation Under the Civil Justice Reform Act, MR-803-ICJ, 1996. $20.00.

Lind, E. A., Arbitrating High-Stakes Cases: An Evaluation of Court-Annexed Arbitration in a United States District Court, R-3809-ICJ, 1990. $10.00.

Lind, E. A., R. J. MacCoun, P. A. Ebener, W. L. F. Felstiner, D. R. Hensler, J. Resnik, and T. R. Tyler, The Perception of Justice: Tort Litigants' Views of Trial, Court-Annexed Arbitration, and Judicial Settlement Conferences, R-3708-ICJ, 1989. $7.50.

MacCoun, R. J., Unintended Consequences of Court Arbitration: A Cautionary Tale from New Jersey, RP-134, 1992. (Reprinted from The Justice System Journal, Vol. 14, No. 2, 1991.) Free.

MacCoun, R. J., E. A. Lind, D. R. Hensler, D. L. Bryant, and P. A. Ebener, Alternative Adjudication: An Evaluation of the New Jersey Automobile Arbitration Program, R-3676-ICJ, 1988. $10.00.

MacCoun, R. J., E. A. Lind, and T. R. Tyler, Alternative Dispute Resolution in Trial and Appellate Courts, RP-117, 1992. (Reprinted from Handbook of Psychology and Law, 1992.) Free.

Moller, E., E. S. Rolph, and P. Ebener, *Private Dispute Resolution in the Banking Industry*, MR-259-ICJ, 1993. $13.00.

Resnik, J., *Many Doors? Closing Doors? Alternative Dispute Resolution and Adjudication,* RP-439, 1995. (Reprinted from *The Ohio State Journal on Dispute Resolution,* Vol. 10, No. 2, 1995.) Free.

Rolph, E. S., *Introducing Court-Annexed Arbitration: A Policymaker's Guide,* R-3167-ICJ, 1984. $10.00.

Rolph, E. S., and D. R. Hensler, *Court-Ordered Arbitration: The California Experience,* N-2186-ICJ, 1984. $4.00.

Rolph, E. S., and E. Moller, *Evaluating Agency Alternative Dispute Resolution Programs: A Users' Guide to Data Collection and Use,* MR-534-ACUS/ICJ, 1995. $13.00.

Rolph, E. S., E. Moller, and L. Petersen, *Escaping the Courthouse: Private Alternative Dispute Resolution in Los Angeles,* MR-472-JRHD/ICJ, 1994. $15.00.

Special Issues

Kakalik, J. S., D. R. Hensler, D. McCaffrey, M. Oshiro, N. M. Pace, and M. E. Vaiana, *Discovery Management: Further Analysis of the Civil Justice Reform Act Evaluation Data,* MR-941-ICJ, 1997. $15.00.

Kritzer, H. M., W. L. F. Felstiner, A. Sarat, and D. M. Trubek, *The Impact of Fee Arrangement on Lawyer Effort,* P-7180-ICJ, 1986. $4.00.

Priest, G. L., *Regulating the Content and Volume of Litigation: An Economic Analysis,* R-3084-ICJ, 1983. $4.00.

Priest, G. L., and B. Klein, *The Selection of Disputes for Litigation,* R-3032-ICJ, 1984. $7.50.

Resnik, J., *Managerial Judges,* R-3002-ICJ, 1982. (Reprinted from the *Harvard Law Review,* Vol. 96, No. 374, December 1982.) $7.50.

———, *Failing Faith: Adjudicatory Procedure in Decline*, P-7272-ICJ, 1987. (Reprinted from the *University of Chicago Law Review*, Vol. 53, No. 2, 1986.) $7.50.

———, *Due Process: A Public Dimension*, P-7418-ICJ, 1988. (Reprinted from the *University of Florida Law Review*, Vol. 39, No. 2, 1987.) $4.00.

———, *Judging Consent*, P-7419-ICJ, 1988. (Reprinted from the *University of Chicago Legal Forum*, Vol. 1987.) $7.50.

———, *From "Cases" to "Litigation,"* RP-110, 1992. (Reprinted from *Law and Contemporary Problems*, Vol. 54, No. 3, Summer 1991.) Free.

———, *Whose Judgment? Vacating Judgments, Preferences for Settlement, and the Role of Adjudication at the Close of the Twentieth Century*, RP-364, 1995. (Reprinted from *UCLA Law Review*, Vol. 41, No. 6, August 1994.) Free.

Waterman, D. A., and M. A. Peterson, *Evaluating Civil Claims: An Expert Systems Approach,* P-7073-ICJ, March 1985. $4.00.

———, *Models of Legal Decisionmaking,* R-2717-ICJ, 1981. $4.00.

AREAS OF LIABILITY

Auto Personal Injury Compensation

Abrahamse, A., and S. J. Carroll, *The Effects of a Choice Auto Insurance Plan on Insurance Costs*, MR-540-ICJ, 1995. $13.00.

———, *The Effects of a Choice Automobile Insurance Plan Under Consideration by the Joint Economic Committee of the United States Congress,* DRU-1609-ICJ, April 1997. Free.

Carroll, S. J., *Effects of an Auto-Choice Automobile Insurance Plan on Costs and Premiums,* CT-141-1, March 1997. (Written statement delivered on March 19, 1997, to the Joint Economic Committee of the United States Congress.) $5.00.

———, *Effects of a Choice Automobile Insurance Plan on Costs and Premiums: Testimony Presented to the Senate Commerce, Science, and Transportation Committee, July 1997,* CT-144, July 1997. (Written statement delivered on July 17, 1997, to the Commerce, Science, and Transportation Committee of the United States Senate.) $5.00.

Carroll, S. J., and A. Abrahamse, *The Effects of a Proposed No-Fault Plan on the Costs of Auto Insurance in California: An Updated Analysis,* IP-146-1, January 1996. Free.

———, *The Effects of a Choice Automobile Insurance Plan on Insurance Costs and Compensation: An Updated Analysis,* MR-970-ICJ, 1998. $9.00

———, *The Effects of Proposition 213 on the Costs of Auto Insurance in California,* IP-157, September 1996. Free.

Carroll, S. J., and J. S. Kakalik, *No-Fault Approaches to Compensating Auto Accident Victims,* RP-229, 1993. (Reprinted from *The Journal of Risk and Insurance*, Vol. 60, No. 2, 1993.) Free.

Carroll, S. J., A. Abrahamse, and M. E. Vaiana, *The Costs of Excess Medical Claims for Automobile Personal Injuries*, DB-139-ICJ, 1995. $6.00.

Carroll, S. J., J. S. Kakalik, N. M. Pace, and J. L. Adams, *No-Fault Approaches to Compensating People Injured in Automobile Accidents*, R-4019-ICJ, 1991. $20.00.

Carroll, S. J., and J. S. Kakalik, with D. Adamson, *No-Fault Automobile Insurance: A Policy Perspective*, R-4019/1-ICJ, 1991. $4.00.

Hammitt, J. K., *Automobile Accident Compensation, Volume II, Payments by Auto Insurers*, R-3051-ICJ, 1985. $10.00.

Hammitt, J. K., and J. E. Rolph, *Limiting Liability for Automobile Accidents: Are No-Fault Tort Thresholds Effective?* N-2418-ICJ, 1985. $4.00.

Hammitt, J. K., R. L. Houchens, S. S. Polin, and J. E. Rolph, *Automobile Accident Compensation: Volume IV, State Rules*, R-3053-ICJ, 1985. $7.50.

Houchens, R. L., *Automobile Accident Compensation: Volume III, Payments from All Sources*, R-3052-ICJ, 1985. $7.50.

MacCoun, R. J., E. A. Lind, D. R. Hensler, D. L. Bryant, and P. A. Ebener, *Alternative Adjudication: An Evaluation of the New Jersey Automobile Arbitration Program*, R-3676-ICJ, 1988. $10.00.

O'Connell, J., S. J. Carroll, M. Horowitz, and A. Abrahamse, *Consumer Choice in the Auto Insurance Market*, RP-254, 1994. (Reprinted from the *Maryland Law Review*, Vol. 52, 1993.) Free.

O'Connell, J., S. J. Carroll, M. Horowitz, A. F. Abrahamse, and P. Jamieson, *The Comparative Costs of Allowing Consumer Choice for Auto Insurance in All Fifty States,* RP-518, 1996. Free.

O'Connell, J., S. J. Carroll, M. Horowitz, A. Abrahamse, and D. Kaiser, *The Costs of Consumer Choice for Auto Insurance in States Without No-Fault Insurance*, RP-442, 1995. (Reprinted from *Maryland Law Review*, Vol. 54, No. 2, 1995.) Free.

Rolph, J. E., with J. K. Hammitt, R. L. Houchens, and S. S. Polin, *Automobile Accident Compensation: Volume I, Who Pays How Much How Soon?* R-3050-ICJ, 1985. $4.00.

Asbestos

Hensler, D. R., *Resolving Mass Toxic Torts: Myths and Realities*, P-7631-ICJ, 1990. (Reprinted from the *University of Illinois Law Review*, Vol. 1989, No. 1, 1989.) $4.00.

———, *Asbestos Litigation in the United States: A Brief Overview*, P-7776-ICJ, 1992. (Testimony before the Courts and Judicial Administration Subcommittee, United States House Judiciary Committee, October 1991.) $4.00.

———, Assessing Claims Resolution Facilities: What We Need to Know, RP-107, 1992. (Reprinted from Law and Contemporary Problems, Vol. 53, No. 4, Autumn 1990.) Free.

———, Fashioning a National Resolution of Asbestos Personal Injury Litigation: A Reply to Professor Brickman, RP-114, 1992. (Reprinted from Cardozo Law Review, Vol. 13, No. 6, April 1992.) Free.

Hensler, D. R., W. L. F. Felstiner, M. Selvin, and P. A. Ebener, Asbestos in the Courts: The Challenge of Mass Toxic Torts, R-3324-ICJ, 1985. $10.00.

Kakalik, J. S., P. A. Ebener, W. L. F. Felstiner, and M. G. Shanley, Costs of Asbestos Litigation, R-3042-ICJ, 1983. $4.00.

Kakalik, J. S., P. A. Ebener, W. L. F. Felstiner, G. W. Haggstrom, and M. G. Shanley, Variation in Asbestos Litigation Compensation and Expenses, R-3132-ICJ, 1984. $7.50.

Peterson, M. A., Giving Away Money: Comparative Comments on Claims Resolution Facilities, RP-108, 1992. (Reprinted from Law and Contemporary Problems, Vol. 53, No. 4, Autumn 1990.) Free.

Peterson, M. A., and M. Selvin, Resolution of Mass Torts: Toward a Framework for Evaluation of Aggregative Procedures, N-2805-ICJ, 1988. $7.50.

———, Mass Justice: The Limited and Unlimited Power of Courts, RP-116, 1992. (Reprinted from Law and Contemporary Problems, No. 3, Summer 1991.) Free.

Selvin, M., and L. Picus, The Debate over Jury Performance: Observations from a Recent Asbestos Case, R-3479-ICJ, 1987. $10.00.

Aviation Accidents

Kakalik, J. S., E. M. King, M. Traynor, P. A. Ebener, and L. Picus, *Costs and Compensation Paid in Aviation Accident Litigation,* R-3421-ICJ, 1988. $10.00.

———, *Aviation Accident Litigation Survey: Data Collection Forms*, N-2773-ICJ, 1988. $7.50.

King, E. M., and J. P. Smith, *Computing Economic Loss in Cases of Wrongful Death,* R-3549-ICJ, 1988. $10.00.

———, *Economic Loss and Compensation in Aviation Accidents*, R-3551-ICJ, 1988. $10.00.

———, *Dispute Resolution Following Airplane Crashes*, R-3585-ICJ, 1988. $7.50.

———,*Executive Summaries of the Aviation Accident Study*, R-3684, 1988. $7.50.

Environment: California's Clean-Air Strategy

Dixon, L. S., and S. Garber, California's Ozone-Reduction Strategy for Light-Duty Vehicles: Direct Costs, Direct Emission Effects and Market Responses, MR-695-ICJ, 1996. $13.00.

———, Economic Perspectives on Revising California's Zero-Emission Vehicle Mandate, CT-137, March 1996. $5.00.

Dixon, L. S., S. Garber, and M. E. Vaiana, California's Ozone-Reduction Strategy for Light-Duty Vehicles: An Economic Assessment, MR-695/1-ICJ, 1996. $15.00.

———, Making ZEV Policy Despite Uncertainty: An Annotated Briefing for the California Air Resources Board, DRU-1266-1-ICJ, 1995. Free.

Environment: Superfund

Acton, J. P., *Understanding Superfund: A Progress Report*, R-3838-ICJ, 1989. $7.50.
40

Acton, J. P., and L. S. Dixon with D. Drezner, L. Hill, and S. McKenney, *Superfund and Transaction Costs: The Experiences of Insurers and Very Large Industrial Firms*, R-4132-ICJ, 1992. $7.50.

Dixon, L. S., *RAND Research on Superfund Transaction Costs: A Summary of Findings to Date,* CT-111, November 1993. $5.00.

———, *Fixing Superfund: The Effect of the Proposed Superfund Reform Act of 1994 on Transaction Costs*, MR-455-ICJ, 1994. $15.00.

———, *Superfund and Transaction Costs: The Experiences of Insurers and Very Large Industrial Firms,* CT-102, 1992. $5.00.

———, *Superfund Liability Reform: Implications for Transaction Costs and Site Cleanup*, CT-125, 1995. $5.00.

Dixon, L. S., D. S. Drezner, and J. K. Hammitt, *Private-Sector Cleanup Expenditures and Transaction Costs at 18 Superfund Sites*, MR-204-EPA/RC, 1993. $13.00.

Reuter, P., *The Economic Consequences of Expanded Corporate Liability: An Exploratory Study*, N-2807-ICJ, 1988. $7.50.

Law and the Changing American Workplace

Darling-Hammond, L., and T. J. Kniesner, *The Law and Economics of Workers' Compensation*, R-2716-ICJ, 1980. $7.50.

Dertouzos, J. N., E. Holland, and P. A. Ebener, *The Legal and Economic Consequences of Wrongful Termination*, R-3602-ICJ, 1988. $7.50.

Dertouzos, J. N., and L. A. Karoly, *Labor-Market Responses to Employer Liability*, R-3989-ICJ, 1992. $7.50.

Marquis, M. S., *Economic Consequences of Work-Related Injuries,* CT-103, 1992. $5.00.

Peterson, Mark A., Robert T. Reville, and Rachel Kaganoff Stern, with Peter Barth, *Compensating Permanent Workplace Injuries: A Study of the California System,* MR-920-ICJ, 1997. $20.00.

Stern, Rachel Kaganoff, Mark A. Peterson, Robert T. Reville, and Mary E. Vaiana, *Findings and Recommendations on California's Permanent Partial Disability System: Executive Summary,* MR-919-ICJ, 1997. $8.00.

Victor, R. B., *Workers' Compensation and Workplace Safety: The Nature of Employer Financial Incentives*, R-2979-ICJ, 1982. $7.50.

Victor, R. B., L. R. Cohen, and C. E. Phelps, *Workers' Compensation and Workplace Safety: Some Lessons from Economic Theory*, R-2918-ICJ, 1982. $7.50.

Medical Malpractice

Bailis, D. S., and R. J. MacCoun, *Estimating Liability Risks with the Media as Your Guide,* RP-606, 1996. (Reprinted from *Law and Human Behavior,* Vol. 20, No. 4, 1996, pp. 419–429.) Free.

Danzon, P. M., *Contingent Fees for Personal Injury Litigation*, R-2458-HCFA, 1980. $4.00.

———, *The Disposition of Medical Malpractice Claims*, R-2622-HCFA, 1980. $7.50.

———, *Why Are Malpractice Premiums So High—Or So Low?* R-2623-HCFA, 1980. $4.00.

———, *The Frequency and Severity of Medical Malpractice Claims*, R-2870-ICJ/HCFA, 1982. $7.50.

———, *New Evidence on the Frequency and Severity of Medical Malpractice Claims*, R-3410-ICJ, 1986. $4.00.

———,*The Effects of Tort Reform son the Frequency and Severity of Medical Malpractice Claims: A Summary of Research Results*, P-7211-ICJ, 1986. (Testimony before the Committee on the Judiciary, United States Senate, March 1986.) $4.00.

Danzon, P. M., and L. A. Lillard, *The Resolution of Medical Malpractice Claims: Modeling the Bargaining Process*, R-2792-ICJ, 1982. $7.50.

———, *Settlement Out of Court: The Disposition of Medical Malpractice Claims*, P-6800, 1982. $4.00.

———,*The Resolution of Medical Malpractice Claims: Research Results and Policy Implications*, R-2793-ICJ, 1982. $4.00.

Kravitz, R. L. , J. E. Rolph, and K. A. McGuigan, *Malpractice Claims Data as a Quality Improvement Tool: I. Epidemiology of Error in Four Specialties*, N-3448/1-RWJ, 1991. $4.00.

Lewis, E., and J. E. Rolph, The Bad Apples? Malpractice Claims Experience of Physicians with a Surplus Lines Insurer, P-7812, 1993. $4.00.

Rolph, E. S., Health Care Delivery and Tort: Systems on a Collision Course? Conference Proceedings, Dallas, June 1991, N-3524-ICJ, 1992. $10.00.

Rolph, J. E., Some Statistical Evidence on Merit Rating in Medical Malpractice Insurance, N-1725-HHS, 1981. $4.00.

———, Merit Rating for Physicians' Malpractice Premiums: Only a Modest Deterrent, N-3426-MT/RWJ/RC, 1991. $4.00.

Rolph, J. E., R. L. Kravitz, and K. A. McGuigan, Malpractice Claims Data as a Quality Improvement Tool: II. Is Targeting Effective? N-3448/2-RWJ, 1991. $4.00.

Williams, A. P., Malpractice, Outcomes, and Appropriateness of Care, P-7445, May 1988. $4.00.

Product Liability

Bailis, D. S., and R. J. MacCoun, *Estimating Liability Risks with the Media as Your Guide,* RP-606, 1996. (Reprinted from *Law and Human Behavior,* Vol. 20, No. 4, 1996, pp. 419–429.) Free.

Dunworth, T., *Product Liability and the Business Sector: Litigation Trends in Federal Courts*, R-3668-ICJ, 1988. $7.50.

Eads, G., and P. Reuter, *Designing Safer Products: Corporate Responses to Product Liability Law and Regulation*, R-3022-ICJ, 1983. $15.00.

———, *Designing Safer Products: Corporate Responses to Product Liability Law and Regulation*, P-7089-ICJ, 1985. (Reprinted from the *Journal of Product Liability*, Vol. 7, 1985.) $4.00.

Garber, S., *Product Liability and the Economics of Pharmaceuticals and Medical Devices*, R-4285-ICJ, 1993. $15.00.

Hensler, D. R., *Summary of Research Results on Product Liability*, P-7271-ICJ, 1986. (Statement submitted to the Committee on the Judiciary, United States Senate, October 1986.) $4.00.

———, *What We Know and Don't Know About Product Liability*, P-7775-ICJ, 1993. (Statement submitted to the Commerce Committee, United States Senate, September 1991.) $4.00.

Moller, E., *Trends in Civil Jury Verdicts Since 1985,* MR-694-ICJ, 1996. $15.00.

Peterson, M. A., *Civil Juries in the 1980s: Trends in Jury Trials and Verdicts in California and Cook County, Illinois*, R-3466-ICJ, 1987. $7.50.

Reuter, P., *The Economic Consequences of Expanded Corporate Liability: An Exploratory Study*, N-2807-ICJ, 1988. $7.50.

Punitive Damages

Carroll, S. J., *Punitive Damages in Financial Injury Jury Verdicts,* CT-143, June 1997. (Written statement delivered on June 24, 1997, to the Judiciary Committee of the United States Senate.) $5.00.

Garber, S., *Product Liability and the Economics of Pharmaceuticals and Medical Devices*, R-4285-ICJ, 1993. $15.00.

Hensler, D. R., and E. Moller, *Trends in Punitive Damages: Preliminary Data from Cook County, Illinois, and San Francisco, California,* DRU-1014-ICJ, 1995. Free.

Kakalik, J. S., P. A. Ebener, W. L. F. Felstiner, G. W. Haggstrom, and M. G. Shanley, *Variation in Asbestos Litigation Compensation and Expenses*, R-3132-ICJ, 1984. $7.50.

MacCoun, R. J., *Inside the Black Box: What Empirical Research Tells Us About Decisionmaking by Civil Juries*, RP-238, 1993. (Reprinted from Robert E. Litan, ed., *Verdict: Assessing the Civil Jury System*, The Brookings Institution, 1993.) Free.

Moller, E., *Trends in Civil Jury Verdicts Since 1985,* MR-694-ICJ, 1996. $15.00.

———, *Trends in Punitive Damages: Preliminary Data from California,* DRU-1059-ICJ, 1995. Free.

Moller, E., N. M. Pace, and S. J. Carroll, *Punitive Damages in Financial Injury Jury Verdicts,* MR-888-ICJ, 1997. $9.00.

———, *Punitive Damages in Financial Injury Jury Verdicts: Executive Summary,* MR-889-ICJ, 1997. $15.00.

Moller, E., E. S. Rolph, and P. Ebener, *Private Dispute Resolution in the Banking Industry*, MR-259-ICJ, 1993. $13.00.

Peterson, M. A., *Punitive Damages: Preliminary Empirical Findings*, N-2342-ICJ, 1985. $4.00.

Peterson, M. A., S. Sarma, and M. G. Shanley, *Punitive Damages: Empirical Findings*, R-3311-ICJ, 1987. $7.50.

Selvin, M., and L. Picus, The Debate over Jury Performance: Observations from a Recent Asbestos Case, R-3479-ICJ, 1987. $10.00.

Shubert, G. H., Some Observations on the Need for Tort Reform, P-7189-ICJ, 1986. (Testimony before the National Conference of State Legislatures, January 1986.) $4.00.

MASS TORTS AND CLASS ACTIONS

Hensler, D. R., *Resolving Mass Toxic Torts: Myths and Realities*, P-7631-ICJ, 1990. (Reprinted from the *University of Illinois Law Review*, Vol. 1989, No. 1.) $4.00.

———, *Asbestos Litigation in the United States: A Brief Overview*, P-7776-ICJ, 1992. (Testimony before the Courts and Judicial Administration Subcommittee, United States House Judiciary Committee, October 1991.) $4.00.

———, *Assessing Claims Resolution Facilities: What We Need to Know*, RP-107, 1992. (Reprinted from *Law and Contemporary Problems*, Vol. 53, No. 4, Autumn 1990.) Free.

———, *Fashioning a National Resolution of Asbestos Personal Injury Litigation: A Reply to Professor Brickman*, RP-114, 1992. (Reprinted from *Cardozo Law Review*, Vol. 13, No. 6, April 1992.) Free.

———, *A Glass Half Full, a Glass Half Empty: The Use of Alternative Dispute Resolution in Mass Personal Injury Litigation*, RP-446, 1995. (Reprinted from *Texas Law Review*, Vol. 73, No. 7, June 1995.) Free.

Hensler, D. R., W. L. F. Felstiner, M. Selvin, and P. A. Ebener, *Asbestos in the Courts: The Challenge of Mass Toxic Torts*, R-3324-ICJ, 1985. $10.00.

Hensler, D. R., J. Gross, E. Moller, and N. Pace, *Preliminary Results of the RAND Study of Class Action Litigation*, DB-220-ICJ, 1997. $6.00.

Hensler, D. R., and M. A. Peterson, *Understanding Mass Personal Injury Litigation: A Socio-Legal Analysis*, RP-311, 1994. (Reprinted from *Brooklyn Law Review*, Vol. 59, No. 3, Fall 1993.) Free.

Kakalik, J. S., P. A. Ebener, W. L. F. Felstiner, G. W. Haggstrom, and M. G. Shanley, *Variation in Asbestos Litigation Compensation and Expenses*, R-3132-ICJ, 1984. $7.50.

Kakalik, J. S., P. A. Ebener, W. L. F. Felstiner, and M. G. Shanley, *Costs of Asbestos Litigation*, R-3042-ICJ, 1983. $4.00.

Peterson, M. A., *Giving Away Money: Comparative Comments on Claims Resolution Facilities*, RP-108, 1992. (Reprinted from *Law and Contemporary Problems*, Vol. 53, No. 4, Autumn 1990.) Free.

Peterson, M. A., and M. Selvin, *Resolution of Mass Torts: Toward a Framework for Evaluation of Aggregative Procedures*, N-2805-ICJ, 1988. $7.50.

———, *Mass Justice: The Limited and Unlimited Power of Courts*, RP-116, 1992. (Reprinted from *Law and Contemporary Problems*, Vol. 54, No. 3, Summer 1991.) Free.

Selvin, M., and L. Picus, *The Debate over Jury Performance: Observations from a Recent Asbestos Case*, R-3479-ICJ, 1987. $10.00.

Resnik, J., D. E. Curtis, and D. R. Hensler, *Individuals Within the Aggregate: Relationships, Representation, and Fees*, RP-584, 1996. (Reprinted from *New York University Law Review*, Vol. 71, Nos. 1–2, April–May 1996.) Free

TRENDS IN THE TORT LITIGATION SYSTEM

Carroll, S. J., *Punitive Damages in Financial Injury Jury Verdicts,* CT-143, June 1997. (Written statement delivered on June 24, 1997, to the Judiciary Committee of the United States Senate.) $5.00

Galanter, M., B. Garth, D. Hensler, and F. K. Zemans, *How to Improve Civil Justice Policy,* RP-282. (Reprinted from *Judicature*, Vol. 77, No. 4, January/February 1994.) Free.

Hensler, D. R., *Summary of Research Results on the Tort Liability System,* P-7210-ICJ, 1986. (Testimony before the Committee on Commerce, Science, and Transportation, United States Senate, February 1986.) $4.00.

———, *Trends in California Tort Liability Litigation*, P-7287-ICJ, 1987. (Testimony before the Select Committee on Insurance, California State Assembly, October 1987.) $4.00.

———, *Reading the Tort Litigation Tea Leaves: What's Going on in the Civil Liability System?* RP-226. (Reprinted from *The Justice System Journal*, Vol. 16, No. 2, 1993.) Free.

———, *A Glass Half Full, a Glass Half Empty: The Use of Alternative Dispute Resolution in Mass Personal Injury Litigation*, RP-446, 1995. (Reprinted from *Texas Law Review*, Vol. 73, No. 7, June 1995.) Free..

Hensler, D. R., and E. Moller, *Trends in Punitive Damages: Preliminary Data from Cook County, Illinois, and San Francisco, California,* DRU-1014-ICJ, 1995. Free.

Hensler, D. R., M. E. Vaiana, J. S. Kakalik, and M. A. Peterson, *Trends in Tort Litigation: The Story Behind the Statistics*, R-3583-ICJ, 1987. $4.00.

Kakalik, J. S., D. R. Hensler, D. McCaffrey, M. Oshiro, N. M. Pace, and M. E. Vaiana, *Discovery Management: Further Analysis of the Civil Justice Reform Act Evaluation Data,* MR-941-ICJ, 1997. $15.00.

Moller, E., Trends in Punitive Damages: Preliminary Data from California, DRU-1059-ICJ, 1995. Free.

———, Trends in Civil Jury Verdicts Since 1985, MR-694-ICJ, 1996. $15.00.

Moller, E., N. M. Pace, and S. J. Carroll, Punitive Damages in Financial Injury Jury Verdicts, MR-888-ICJ, 1997. $9.00.

———, Punitive Damages in Financial Injury Jury Verdicts: Executive Summary, MR-889-ICJ, 1997. $15.00.

Peterson, M. A., Summary of Research Results: Trends and Patterns in Civil Jury Verdicts, P-7222-ICJ, 1986. (Testimony before the Subcommittee on Oversight, Committee on Ways and Means, United States House of Representatives, March 1986.) $4.00.

———, Civil Juries in the 1980s: Trends in Jury Trials and Verdicts in California and Cook County, Illinois, R-3466-ICJ, 1987. $7.50.

Peterson, M. A., and G. L. Priest, The Civil Jury: Trends in Trials and Verdicts, Cook County, Illinois, 1960–1979, R-2881-ICJ, 1982. $7.50.

ECONOMIC EFFECTS OF THE LIABILITY SYSTEM

General

Carroll, S. J., A. Abrahamse, M. S. Marquis, and M. E. Vaiana, *Liability System Incentives to Consume Excess Medical Care*, DRU-1264-ICJ, 1995. Free.

Johnson, L. L., *Cost-Benefit Analysis and Voluntary Safety Standards for Consumer Products*, R-2882-ICJ, 1982. $7.50.

Reuter, P., *The Economic Consequences of Expanded Corporate Liability: An Exploratory Study*, N-2807-ICJ, 1988. $7.50.

Product Liability

Bailis, D. S., and R. J. MacCoun, *Estimating Liability Risks with the Media as Your Guide*, RP-606, 1996. (Reprinted from *Law and Human Behavior,* Vol. 20, No. 4, 1996, pp. 419–429.) Free.

Dunworth, T., *Product Liability and the Business Sector: Litigation Trends in Federal Courts,* R-3668-ICJ, 1988. $7.50.

Eads, G., and P. Reuter, *Designing Safer Products: Corporate Responses to Product Liability Law and Regulation,* R-3022-ICJ, 1983. $15.00.

———, Designing Safer Products: Corporate Responses to Product Liability Law and Regulation, P-7089-ICJ, 1985. (Reprinted from Journal of Product Liability, Vol. 7, 1985.) $4.00.

Garber, S., Product Liability and the Economics of Pharmaceuticals and Medical Devices, R-4285-ICJ, 1993. $15.00.

Hensler, D. R., Summary of Research Results on Product Liability, P-7271-ICJ, 1986. (Statement submitted to the Committee on the Judiciary, United States Senate, October 1986.) $4.00.

———, What We Know and Don't Know About Product Liability, P-7775-ICJ, 1993. (Statement submitted to the Commerce Committee, United States Senate, September 1991.) $4.00.

Peterson, M. A., Civil Juries in the 1980s: Trends in Jury Trials and Verdicts in California and Cook County, Illinois, R-3466-ICJ, 1987. $7.50.

Punitive Damages

Carroll, S. J., *Punitive Damages in Financial Injury Jury Verdicts,* CT-143, June 1997. (Written statement delivered on June 24, 1997, to the Judiciary Committee of the United States Senate.) $5.00.

Garber, S., *Product Liability and the Economics of Pharmaceuticals and Medical Devices*, R-4285-ICJ, 1993. $15.00.

Hensler, D. R., and E. Moller, *Trends in Punitive Damages: Preliminary Data from Cook County, Illinois, and San Francisco, California,* DRU-1014-ICJ, 1995. Free.

Kakalik, J. S., P. A. Ebener, W. L. F. Felstiner, G. W. Haggstrom, and M. G. Shanley, *Variation in Asbestos Litigation Compensation and Expenses*, R-3132-ICJ, 1984. $7.50.

MacCoun, R. J., *Inside the Black Box: What Empirical Research Tells Us About Decisionmaking by Civil Juries*, RP-238, 1993. (Reprinted from Robert E. Litan, ed., *Verdict: Assessing the Civil Jury System*, The Brookings Institution, 1993.) Free.

Moller, E., *Trends in Civil Jury Verdicts Since 1985,* MR-694-ICJ, 1996. $15.00.

———, *Trends in Punitive Damages: Preliminary Data from California,* DRU-1059-ICJ, 1995. Free.

Moller, E., N. M. Pace, and S. J. Carroll, *Punitive Damages in Financial Injury Jury Verdicts,* MR-888-ICJ, 1997. $9.00.

———, *Punitive Damages in Financial Injury Jury Verdicts: Executive Summary,* MR-889-ICJ, 1997. $15.00.

Moller, E., E. S. Rolph, and P. Ebener, *Private Dispute Resolution in the Banking Industry*, MR-259-ICJ, 1993. $13.00.

Peterson, M. A., Punitive Damages: Preliminary Empirical Findings, N-2342-ICJ, 1985. $4.00.

Peterson, M. A., S. Sarma, and M. G. Shanley, Punitive Damages: Empirical Findings, R-3311-ICJ, 1987. $7.50.

Selvin, M., and L. Picus, The Debate over Jury Performance: Observations from a Recent Asbestos Case, R-3479-ICJ, 1987. $10.00.

Shubert, G. H., Some Observations on the Need for Tort Reform, P-7189-ICJ, 1986. (Testimony before the National Conference of State Legislatures, January 1986.) $4.00.

Law and the Changing American Workplace

Darling-Hammond, L., and T. J. Kniesner, *The Law and Economics of Workers' Compensation*, R-2716-ICJ, 1980. $7.50.

Dertouzos, J. N., E. Holland, and P. A. Ebener, *The Legal and Economic Consequences of Wrongful Termination*, R-3602-ICJ, 1988. $7.50.

Dertouzos, J. N., and L. A. Karoly, *Labor-Market Responses to Employer Liability*, R-3989-ICJ, 1992. $7.50.

Marquis, M. S., *Economic Consequences of Work-Related Injuries,* CT-103, 1992. $5.00.

Peterson, Mark A., Robert T. Reville, and Rachel Kaganoff Stern, with Peter Barth, *Compensating Permanent Workplace Injuries: A Study of the California System,* MR-920-ICJ, 1997. $20.00.

Stern, Rachel Kaganoff, Mark A. Peterson, Robert T. Reville, and Mary E. Vaiana, *Findings and Recommendations on California's Permanent Partial Disability System: Executive Summary,* MR-919-ICJ, 1997. $8.00.

Victor, R. B., *Workers' Compensation and Workplace Safety: The Nature of Employer Financial Incentives*, R-2979-ICJ, 1982. $7.50.

Victor, R. B., L. R. Cohen, and C. E. Phelps, *Workers' Compensation and Workplace Safety: Some Lessons from Economic Theory*, R-2918-ICJ, 1982. $7.50.

COMPENSATION SYSTEMS

System Design

Darling-Hammond, L., and T. J. Kniesner, *The Law and Economics of Workers' Compensation*, R-2716-ICJ, 1980. $7.50.

Hammitt, J. K., R. L. Houchens, S. S. Polin, and J. E. Rolph, *Automobile Accident Compensation: Volume IV, State Rules*, R-3053-ICJ, 1985. $7.50.

Hammitt, J. K., and J. E. Rolph, *Limiting Liability for Automobile Accidents: Are No-Fault Tort Thresholds Effective?* N-2418-ICJ, 1985. $4.00.

Hensler, D. R., *Resolving Mass Toxic Torts: Myths and Realities*, P-7631-ICJ, 1990. (Reprinted from the *University of Illinois Law Review*, Vol. 1989, No. 1, 1989.) $4.00.

———, *Assessing Claims Resolution Facilities: What We Need to Know*, RP-107, 1992. (Reprinted from *Law and Contemporary Problems*, Vol. 53, No. 4, Autumn 1990.) Free.

King, E. M., and J. P. Smith, *Computing Economic Loss in Cases of Wrongful Death,* R-3549-ICJ, 1988. $10.00.

Peterson, M. A., and M. Selvin, *Resolution of Mass Torts: Toward a Framework for Evaluation of Aggregative Procedures*, N-2805-ICJ, 1988. $7.50.

Rolph, E. S., *Framing the Compensation Inquiry*, RP-115, 1992. (Reprinted from the *Cardozo Law Review*, Vol. 13, No. 6, April 1992.) Free.

Victor, R. B., *Workers' Compensation and Workplace Safety: The Nature of Employer Financial Incentives*, R-2979-ICJ, 1982. $7.50.

Victor, R. B., L. R. Cohen, and C. E. Phelps, *Workers' Compensation and Workplace Safety: Some Lessons from Economic Theory*, R-2918-ICJ, 1982. $7.50.

Performance

Abrahamse, A., and S. J. Carroll, *The Effects of a Choice Auto Insurance Plan on Insurance Costs*, MR-540-ICJ, 1995. $13.00.

Carroll, S. J., and A. Abrahamse, *The Effects of a Proposed No-Fault Plan on the Costs of Auto Insurance in California: An Updated Analysis,* IP-146-1, January 1996. Free.
49

———, *The Effects of a Choice Automobile Insurance Plan on Insurance Costs and Compensation: An Updated Analysis,* MR-970-ICJ, 1998. $9.00

Carroll, S. J., and J. S. Kakalik, *No-Fault Approaches to Compensating Auto Accident Victims,* RP-229, 1993. (Reprinted from *The Journal of Risk and Insurance*, Vol. 60, No. 2, 1993.) Free.

Carroll, S. J., A. Abrahamse, and M. E. Vaiana, *The Costs of Excess Medical Claims for Automobile Personal Injuries*, DB-139-ICJ, 1995. $6.00.

Carroll, S. J., A. Abrahamse, M. S. Marquis, and M. E. Vaiana, *Liability System Incentives to Consume Excess Medical Care*, DRU-1264-ICJ, 1995. Free.

Carroll, S. J., J. S. Kakalik, N. M. Pace, and J. L. Adams, *No-Fault Approaches to Compensating People Injured in Automobile Accidents*, R-4019-ICJ, 1991. $20.00.

Carroll, S. J., and J. S. Kakalik, with D. Adamson, *No-Fault Automobile Insurance: A Policy Perspective*, R-4019/1-ICJ, 1991. $4.00.

Hensler, D. R., M. S. Marquis, A. Abrahamse, S. H. Berry, P. A. Ebener, E. G. Lewis, E. A. Lind, R. J. MacCoun, W. G. Manning, J. A. Rogowski, and M. E. Vaiana, *Compensation for Accidental Injuries in the United States*, R-3999-HHS/ICJ, 1991. $20.00.

———, *Compensation for Accidental Injuries in the United States: Executive Summary*, R-3999/1-HHS/ICJ, 1991. $4.00.

———, *Compensation for Accidental Injuries: Research Design and Methods*, N-3230-HHS/ICJ, 1991. $15.00.

King, E. M., and J. P. Smith, *Economic Loss and Compensation in Aviation Accidents*, R-3551-ICJ, 1988. $10.00.

O'Connell, J., S. J. Carroll, M. Horowitz, and A. Abrahamse, *Consumer Choice in the Auto Insurance Market*, RP-254, 1994. (Reprinted from the *Maryland Law Review*, Vol. 52, 1993.) Free.

O'Connell, J., S. J. Carroll, M. Horowitz, A. Abrahamse, and D. Kaiser, *The Costs of Consumer Choice for Auto Insurance in States Without No-Fault Insurance*, RP-442, 1995. (Reprinted from *Maryland Law Review*, Vol. 54, No. 2, 1995.) Free.

Peterson, M. A., *Giving Away Money: Comparative Comments on Claims Resolution Facilities*, RP-108, 1992. (Reprinted from *Law and Contemporary Problems*, Vol. 53, No. 4, Autumn 1990.) Free.

Peterson, M. A., and M. Selvin, *Mass Justice: The Limited and Unlimited Power of Courts*, RP-116, 1992. (Reprinted from *Law and Contemporary Problems*, Vol. 54, No. 3, Summer 1991.) Free.

Peterson, Mark A., Robert T. Reville, and Rachel Kaganoff Stern, with Peter Barth, *Compensating Permanent Workplace Injuries: A Study of the California System,* MR-920-ICJ, 1997. $20.00.

Rolph, J. E., with J. K. Hammitt, R. L. Houchens, and S. S. Polin, *Automobile Accident Compensation: Volume I, Who Pays How Much How Soon?* R-3050-ICJ, 1985. $4.00.

Stern, Rachel Kaganoff, Mark A. Peterson, Robert T. Reville, and Mary E. Vaiana, *Findings and Recommendations on California's Permanent Partial Disability System: Executive Summary,* MR-919-ICJ, 1997. $8.00.

SPECIAL STUDIES

Hensler, D. R., and M. E. Reddy, California Lawyers View the Future: A Report to the Commission on the Future of the Legal Profession and the State Bar, MR-528-ICJ, 1994. $13.00.

Kakalik, J. S., D. R. Hensler, D. McCaffrey, M. Oshiro, N. M. Pace, and M. E. Vaiana, Discovery Management: Further Analysis of the Civil Justice Reform Act Evaluation Data, MR-941-ICJ, 1997. $15.00.

Merz, J. F., and N. M. Pace, Trends in Patent Litigation: The Apparent Influence of Strengthened Patents Attributable to the Court of Appeals for the Federal Circuit, RP-426, 1995. (Reprinted from Journal of the Patent and Trademark Office Society, Vol. 76, No. 8, August 1994.) Free.

An annotated bibliography, CP-253 (1/98), provides a list of RAND publications in the civil justice area through 1997. To request the bibliography or to obtain more information about the Institute for Civil Justice, please write the Institute at this address: The Institute for Civil Justice, RAND, 1700 Main Street, P. O. Box 2138, Santa Monica, California 90407-2138, or call (310) 393-0411, x6916.